Bringing JOY Back into the Classroom

Author
Danny Brassell

Foreword by
Lori Oczkus, Ph.D.

SHELL EDUCATION

Publishing Credits

Dona Herweck Rice, *Editor-in-Chief*; Lee Aucoin, *Creative Director*;
Don Tran, *Print Production Manager*; Timothy J. Bradley, *Illustration Manager*;
Sara Johnson, M.S. Ed., *Senior Editor*; Hillary Wolfe, *Editor*; Juan Chavolla, *Cover Designer*,
Interior Layout Designer; Corinne Burton, M.A. Ed., *Publisher*

Shell Education

5301 Oceanus Drive
Huntington Beach, CA 92649-1030
http://www.shelleducation.com
ISBN 978-1-4258-0756-6
© 2012 Shell Educational Publishing, Inc.
Reprinted 2013

Table of Contents

Foreword

Are you a *"Friday Teacher,"* crawling through the week living for the weekends? Or are you a *"Monday Teacher,"* the kind who looks forward to your work week with excitement and happiness that spills over into your personal life as well? Leave it to the genius of author Danny Brassell to deliver a fresh new take on JOY, an aspect of teaching that can make or break your classroom climate. Although it is a difficult time to be a teacher, *Bringing Joy Back into the Classroom* offers wonderful suggestions for taking control of the atmosphere in your classroom to help you become the most successful, effective teacher possible and to provide an optimal learning environment for your students.

Bringing Joy Back into the Classroom is a career-enhancing book that provides strategies for making teaching more enjoyable even if you are "stuck" in a situation loaded with testing pressures, a contrary staff or administration, challenging students, and an overloaded unrealistic curriculum. If you've ever had the pleasure of hearing Danny Brassell speak you know his rapid fire Robin Williams presentation style is hilariously funny yet realistically down to earth. Lucky for us, Danny's wise humor bounces off the pages of this book, too! Danny's interesting and colorful stories from sports, business, entertainment, and literature help to demonstrate his points in memorable ways making this a professional book you can actually read for enjoyment.

The unique organization of *Bringing Joy Back into the Classroom* focuses on differentiating instruction to reach all students through Abraham Maslow's Hierarchy of Needs (1954)—through their basic to more sophisticated human needs, including physiological, safety, love and belonging, esteem, and self-actualization. Danny borrows from effective motivational strategies used in businesses and other organizations to help us provide optimal learning environments for our students. He sprinkles in classroom creativity, experience, and know-how for the perfect mix of practical ideas to use immediately for results. Each chapter is loaded with ideas you can easily implement in your classroom. Here are just a few of my favorites:

- "Make it a point to improve your AYP, or 'Are you playing?' quotient in your classroom!"

- "Be a thermostat, NOT a thermometer. A thermometer simply measures the temperature conditions while a thermostat sets the temperature and climate of the classroom with caring and high expectations."

- "Stand at the door and 'meet and greet' your students on their way in the classroom. Run morning meetings like a broadcast with an anchor person, weather person, and feature reporters."

- "Try leaving encouraging sticky notes in all sorts of surprising places for students to find such as inside their desks, books, or homework packets."

- "Sometimes give students choices and allow them to help plan lessons. Allow one group to select one of the standards to learn. Another group plans activities while yet another group of students plans the products the class will produce to demonstrate learning."

- "Henry Ford said, 'Whether you believe you can do a thing or not, you are right.' Your students will achieve precisely what you think they will achieve. You will achieve precisely what you think you can achieve."

If your staff tried even just a few of these rich ideas, your student population would thrive and your learning climate would improve. Whether you read this unique guide on your own, with a professional learning community, or with an online community, please join me in thanking Danny Brassell for such a refreshing and much needed book!

Lori Oczkus
Author of *Reciprocal Teaching at Work* and
Interactive Think Aloud Lessons and Literacy Consultant

Preface

Thank you.

Thank you for choosing to teach.

Thank you for choosing to make a difference in children's lives.

When was the last time somebody thanked you for teaching? If you look at any magazine or newspaper lately, everything wrong with society seems to be attributed to teachers. Have you heard that teachers are failing to boost student test scores? Have you heard that teachers aren't teaching their students what is important for them to succeed in the future? There seems to be this popular misconception that teachers receive adequate supplies, ample support, and students from stable environments with tons of parental and community support.

Society is losing too many gifted teachers. You may be one of those teachers who feel overburdened, under-supported, and generally unappreciated. This book is for you. This book is to celebrate you. This book is to remind you why you became a teacher: to engage young minds and feel the joy of making a difference.

Relax, curl up behind this book, and smile.

Are you ready to have fun? Whenever I would say that to my students, they would jump up and shout, "Yeah!" I have been teaching at California State University, Dominguez Hills for over 10 years and in all that time my boss has yet to step into my office and announce, "Today, we're going to have some fun!" I like surrounding myself with positive energy. Our lives are not determined by the socioeconomic status into which we were born, but by the choices we make every day. So, let's choose to be happy and positive, and see what a difference a change in attitude can make!

Dedication

This book is dedicated to Bob Sornson, a great friend, mentor, and colleague, who suggested a couple of years ago that I create a speech that talked about "bringing joy back into the classroom." Contrary to reports in the media, there are a lot of teachers—most, in fact—performing miracles in classrooms every day. Thank you, Bob, for encouraging me to remind teachers how much of a difference they make every day.

This book is based on various presentations I have conducted around the country on motivation, creativity, and differentiated instruction. You can recapture your joy by celebrating the differences of your students. Let me warn you: In an attempt to capture the vibe of those presentations in writing, you may find my writing a little unorthodox. Yes, fun is good. In fact, I think learning has to be fun in order to be meaningful or memorable. When you see me present in person, you will find it easier to follow the book. (Hint: Come to one of my workshops.)

Having taught people of all ages and abilities—from preschoolers to rocket scientists, I have developed a cache of "tricks" to accommodate the vast and varying needs of my audiences, from non-English-speaking immigrant children to prominent executives. One can adapt to the students' needs and ditch strategies that prove ineffective. What works for one student may not work for another. What works this year may be obsolete next year. It is a good idea for teachers to arm themselves with lots of "weapons of mass instruction" in their teaching arsenals, so I hope you find this manual to be a good starting point to provide fresh ideas, reaffirm old ones, and stimulate you to think of better ways to meet the needs of all your learners. As you will see, there is a direct link between differentiating to the various needs of our students and "bringing joy back into the classroom."

I love working with great teachers. They are my heroes. They inspire me. They do what I wish I'd done: stay in the classroom. My biggest regret was leaving the classroom. It took me a long time to get over that. One day, my mother—who is a very peppy person—reminded me that I still have the opportunity to inspire teachers to stay and thrive in the classroom. In this way, I can have an even bigger impact than when I was a teacher. That talk gave me a new perspective, and I take my calling very seriously. My purpose is to help great teachers stay in the classroom. We need you.

Enjoy this book, and remember, you make a difference every day.

—*Danny Brassell*

CHAPTER 1

Introduction

Songs and chants are a fun way to start a class. Each day my students and I write a number of songs and chants. Yes, I sing with middle school and high school students, too. Why? It annoys them (though they secretly enjoy it). And even if songs may annoy some students, they are a great way to help students remember concepts and skills. It also helps to get the blood circulating so that they are not stuck in their seats all day. My students and I try to write songs to basic beats, like nursery rhymes, commercial jingles, TV theme songs, Disney® movies, and the occasional oldies-but-goodies. So, put aside your pride and sing our "Differentiation Ditty":

"The Differentiation Ditty"
By Danny Brassell (2007)
(to the tune of Manfred Mann's "Do Wah Diddy")

There I was just about to teach my class,
Singin', "Do what I say. I'm the teacher. Yes, indeed."
Then my students looked at me en masse,
Askin', "Do what you say? Are you kiddin'? We can't read."
They looked stressed (looked stressed).
They looked bored (looked bored).
They looked stressed. They looked bored.
They were not a happy horde.
I had kids of all sizes. They were different, every one.
Singin', "Do you want to teach a standard or teach me?"
They asked, "Why is school always work, and no fun?"
Sing this: "That is not the way that school has to be!"
I said, "Yes!" (said "Yes!")
"You're all right" (all right).
I said, "Yes! You're all right.
Now our future's lookin' bright."
Our class is now happy, and we learn a lot more.
'Cause we each are different, and we learn differently.
When others critique us, we just shut our door.
And we play. And we sing. And we think critically. Yeah!

There are a number of authors and books that I'd like to recommend. (An extensive recommended reading list is provided in the Appendix, pages 147–150.) Carol Ann Tomlinson is the guru behind differentiated instruction. In fact, she coined the term (1998) and has written numerous books and articles on the subject filled with informative tips for classroom teachers.

Howard Gardner may be one of the most important educational researchers of the past 50 years. I highly recommend all books that consider the learning needs of students based on their multiple intelligences.

Wendy Conklin has written some very practical guides that demonstrate the nitty gritty of how to differentiate any lesson or standard, including *Applying Differentiation Strategies* (2007). Her work is essential reading for anyone interested in specific step-by-step approaches to differentiating instruction.

Finally, all teachers should read a book that far too few American educators know about: *The Learning Revolution* (Dryden and Vos 1994). This is one of the most successful education books of all time. It sold over seven million copies in China alone. It is filled with wonderful ideas about enabling teachers to teach in ways that students will remember. All of these authors' works complement this book in examining better ways to engage students' curiosity so they can think better.

The Joy of Differentiated Instruction

"Differentiated instruction is a teaching philosophy based on the premise that teachers should adapt instruction to student differences. Rather than marching students through the curriculum lockstep, teachers should modify their instruction to meet students' varying readiness levels, learning preferences, and interests. Therefore, the teacher proactively plans a variety of ways to "get at" and express learning."

—Scott Willis and Larry Mann (2000)

"Whenever a teacher reaches out to an individual or small group to vary his or her teaching in order to create the best learning experience possible, that teacher is differentiating instruction."

—Carol Ann Tomlinson (1998)

Basically, Tomlinson, Willis, and Mann agree: one size does not fit all.

In your own seats, or in your own mind, follow these directions:

- Raise your hand if you have a wide diversity of students in your class.

- Raise your hand if you utilize a number of different teaching strategies with your students.

- Raise your hand if you have a hand.

- Repeat after me: "I think, therefore I am." (René Descartes said that.)

- Now, repeat after me: "I think I will succeed, therefore I can." (We said that—just now.)

Whether you're firing up an audience or firing up your students, learning should never be a static activity. School and fun do not have to be mutually exclusive concepts. Learning is a state of mind, and students should be in a positive, joyful state. If you keep students moving and playing, they will be joyful. When students are joyful, they will learn, because they do not even realize that they are learning. How do we get students excited? We pay attention to their individual needs. (Chances are, you are already doing this.) We are all different. We can all learn from somebody else. Wave your arms wildly if you choose to learn from others! Compliment the people in your school and tell them how happy you are to be there. Joy is a state of mind, too, and that starts with you.

Why Is Differentiating Instruction Joyful?

Marilyn Hughes says that "some children need days; some, ten minutes," to learn a particular concept (Gartrell 2010); but, as Willis (2000) observes, "the typical lockstep school schedule ignores this fundamental fact." Really, students are like automobiles: they all require their own type of gasoline, and some students are higher octane than others.

Students come to us with various degrees of readiness. Matching learning opportunities to readiness levels ensures that students will master key skills and understandings rather than glossing over them. (This will be discussed in further detail later.) Additionally, students vary in what interests them and in their learning profiles. By matching learning opportunities to student interests, teachers increase the likelihood that a student sees school as relevant.

Eight Principles of a Differentiated Classroom

Use these principles to guide you (Tomlinson 1998):

 ## Be Clear About What Matters in the Content Area

Know the standards. Adjust instruction so that all students can succeed. Students may meet the standard at different levels, and this is one of the joys in the challenge of teaching—how to help a student progress from reaching the standard at a minimum level to a maximum level.

 ## Understand, Appreciate, and Build Upon Student Differences

Have you ever been visited by a "specialist" who is there to "examine" your students to see if they qualify for Special Education services? How do they test the students? Some of the criteria on the checklists would qualify every student for Special Education, and probably many of the teachers, too. While Special Education is a worthwhile and necessary part of a successful school experience, too many students are improperly labeled or placed in programs simply because they don't fit the mold of the model student.

All students have special needs, and the only labels we should place on students are positive ones, since students tend to rise to our expectations. Treat your students like geniuses, and they will act accordingly. In other words, don't be so quick to judge and dismiss your students. They may surprise you.

 ## Partner Assessment with Instruction

Assessments are more than tests. Assessments are meant to inform and guide instruction. Period. Feedback is more critical than labeling or pigeon-holing kids. There are two types of teachers: The ones who tell students, "You're wrong," and the ones who ask students, "Why did you say that?" Teachers must question students as to how they arrived at their answers. Students are often sophisticated in their reasoning. Their reasoning may simply differ from ours. Understanding this can help us learn better ways to meet their individual learning needs.

I once worked at a preschool where I enjoyed working with a four-year-old named Francisco. One day I showed him the words *Francisco* and *Papá*, and I asked him to point to the word that said "Papá." Francisco pointed to the word *Francisco*, and so I told him he was wrong, right? Wrong! I asked him why he thought that was the word, and he informed me that it was bigger. Hmm, that was interesting. Francisco associated the size of words with the size of people and objects, so of course he thought the longer word, *Francisco*, represented the large image Francisco had of his father. While he may have been technically "wrong," Francisco had shown his teacher a glimpse of how he was thinking. Based on that kind of understanding, any teacher could better serve his needs.

Remember, assess for understanding, to inform instruction, not just at the end of a lesson. Assessment is for the teacher—it provides the justification for the next lesson.

 ## Create a Classroom Community that Honors Learning

Community is everything, and teachers need to build a community of learners in their classrooms. A number of years ago, Dreyer's Ice Cream conducted a study that found three in 10 Americans do not know their neighbors' first and last names. That is completely unacceptable. Students must work together and learn to get along. Do not stand in the front of the classroom all day—sit in the seats beside your students. See the room from their perspectives. Each student has so much to offer. Each is an amazing resource waiting to be discovered.

Additionally, teachers need to "teach to the heart," as the Dalai Lama says. Teachers are not there to make their students smarter. They are there to make them lifelong learners. The world is changing, and people who are willing to investigate and learn new things will have more success adapting to whatever the future holds.

Collaborate with Students in Learning

Ever notice that the landscaping in neighborhoods with high ownership rates is often nicer than on streets with more rentals? Why do you think this is so? Homeowners take better care of their yards because they are more invested. Japanese schools do not employ janitors. Students clean the schools themselves. As a result, their schools are pristine, since no student wants to clean up a big mess. Teachers need to empower their students to take ownership of their classroom. When students see the classroom as belonging to them, they collaborate in making it a better environment. The same goes for assignments. Give students some choices and they will own their work. Ownership fosters pride, diligence, and tenacity. Aren't these the kinds of qualities that will serve our students as they journey through school?

Adjust Content, Process, and Product in Response to Student Readiness, Interests, and Learning Styles

This is known as differentiation. Teaching is like riding a 10-speed bicycle up a hill: You have to shift gears from time to time. Only the stubborn teacher fails to realize the importance of making adjustments. Some subjects lend themselves to easy understanding, while others take a lot more work for the teacher to convey. What kind of knowledge did students have already when they entered the room? Is the lesson relevant to them, or to you? Are you referencing stories, television shows, movies, experiences, or songs that are well-known to them, or foreign? Are the conditions in your room suitable for students to attend to and participate in instruction? How's the noise level outside? How's the lighting inside? Did your students have breakfast this morning? If you have 40 students in your room, there are 40 different reasons why learning may be difficult. Find out, and adjust.

 ## Make Maximum Growth and Continued Success the Goals of a Differentiated Classroom

It should go without saying that teachers differentiate in order to achieve the best results with students. Everything we do needs to be in the interest of student learning.

 ## Stay Flexible (It Is the Hallmark of a Differentiated Classroom)

Good teachers roll with the punches. A colleague told me about a study conducted to see which professionals made the highest number of decisions per hour. Of all professionals, teachers ranked second. Air traffic controllers came in at number one. I would argue that a kindergarten teacher sometimes has a more difficult job than an air traffic controller.

Say you are trying to teach your students how to add 2 + 2.

"Two plus two equals…," you say, before a student yells, "Teacher, can I go to the bathroom?"

You stop to write a bathroom pass. Then you resume your lesson.

"So, two plus two equals…," you say, and then the school secretary knocks on the door and says, "Yo, teacher! You've got a late attendance sheet. You keep on turning in late attendance sheets, and you're going to get late paychecks, you know what I'm saying?" So you apologize and fill in your late attendance sheet. You resume your lesson.

"So, two plus two equals…," you say, and a child from the class next door knocks on the door and asks if students have turned in their pledge sheets for the school's latest fund-raising effort. So you ask students to pass along the sheets, and then you resume your lesson.

"So, two plus two equals…," you say, and then a garbled announcement comes over the intercom, interrupting your lesson again. After taking a moment to try to decode the gibberish, you resume your lesson.

"So, two plus two equals…," you say, and then a parent bursts into the classroom with hands waving, saying, "Maestro, mi hijo no está aquí porque se duele su estomago." You try your best to formulate an answer for her in Spanish before resuming your lesson.

"So, two plus two equals…," you say, and then a cafeteria worker knocks on the door and asks how many students will be eating hot lunch. You do a quick count of student hands before resuming your lesson.

"Okay, kids, two plus two equals three," you say, because you have just lost your mind! Consider everything you just dealt with: students, bureaucracy, and unintelligible intercom speak! No wonder we lose so many teachers in their first three years. We ought to be surprised more are not committed to mental institutions.

Tricks of the Trade

Many teachers fear the word *differentiation* because they are overwhelmed, annoyed, or confused by it. In reality, differentiation is something any good teacher is already striving for, because good teachers constantly adjust their classrooms to meet the needs of different students. To save your sanity, though, take small steps toward implementing systematic differentiation. It takes time to get the hang of it, but once you do, you will probably wonder how you ever taught without differentiating. You and your students will be happier and more productive for it.

Many teachers differentiate the delivery of their instruction without even realizing it. One of the greatest pleasures is watching great teachers. They constantly experiment, refine, and perfect their classroom strategies. When you come across an idea you like, try it out. If it bombs, hold on to it for another day. What bombs today can save you tomorrow.

Teachers should create classrooms that meet state and federal standards. Maintaining high levels of student understanding is accomplished by supporting all students' learning modalities, and by differentiating through content, activities, and product—based on students' readiness, interests, profiles of learning, and environments. Sound like a lot to remember? Use a simple mnemonic trick to help keep differentiation in mind: "Each student is RIPE for learning when the teacher uses his or her thinking CAP." *RIPE* stands for Readiness, Interests, Profiles of Learning, and Environments; *CAP* stands for Content, Activities, and Product (Brassell and Rasinski 2008).

Organization of This Book

This book refocuses teachers on the basics. Abraham Maslow developed his Hierarchy of Needs model for understanding human motivation and personal development. Used extensively in businesses, it provides a great model for teachers to keep in mind when working with students. Indeed, each of us is motivated by these needs. Our most basic needs are inborn, and Maslow attempted to explain how these needs motivate us all. Maslow's original Hierarchy of Needs (Maslow 1954) included five levels, from lower-order needs of physical and emotional well-being to higher-order needs of influence and personal development. They are:

1. Physiological needs (biological needs for basic survival)

2. Safety needs (needs for security and stability)

3. Love and belonging needs (affection and attention from different groups)

4. Esteem needs (status, value, and confidence)

5. Self-actualization needs (a person's need to be and do what the person was born to do)

Maslow's model teaches that we must satisfy each need in turn, beginning with basic survival needs. Only when the lower-order needs of physical and emotional well-being are satisfied can we focus on the higher-order needs of influence and personal development. The remainder of this book is organized into five sections based on Maslow's Hierarchy of Needs.

Many of the anecdotes from this book are drawn from movies, newspaper clippings, reports on National Public Radio, personal experiences, my colleagues, my pastor, and online devotionals. The goal of this book is to demonstrate how we can bring joy back into the classroom by differentiating instruction to meet the various needs that drive us and our students.

It is a dark time out there. Public schools—teachers, in particular—have been taking a beating. While policymakers from both parties push their way in front of microphones to announce what is best for the nation's youth, educators find their opinions almost completely ignored. Government mandates have prompted many great teachers to leave the classroom. This must end.

Let there be light! The goal of this book is to get teachers to "lighten up" and remember—you became teachers to make a lasting, positive impact on students. Constantly consider "AYP." (Besides Adequate Yearly Progress, AYP means asking yourself, "Are You Playing?") The intention of this book is to cram some fun down your throats, so beware! People can argue about the quality of schools, funding shortfalls, or any number of other educational issues until they are blue in the face, but one variable stands out as a tried-and-true indicator of student success: quality teachers. Haven't you enjoyed inspirational books and movies about teachers who inspired students to write through poetry, who challenged impoverished students to excel at calculus, and who taught all of their standards through music? Yet how many books or films about teachers tell the story of one who dramatically changed students' lives by following a school district's scripted reading program? Great teachers inspire by being a little unorthodox in their approaches. It is my hope that this book inspires your "unorthodoxy."

Reflection Questions

1. Who was your favorite teacher? What do you remember the most about him or her?

2. What is it that brings you the most joy in the classroom?

3. How could you make a conscious decision to choose joy?

Physiological Needs

Overview

For the most part, physiological needs are fairly obvious; they are the basic biological requirements for survival. If these requirements are not met, humans cannot function.

They provide the essential foundation for all learning to take place. There can be no joy where there is hunger or unrest. In order to create a classroom that feeds souls every day, you first have to be sure the needs of the body are met.

Fifteen Ways to Meet Your Physiological Needs

 Breathe

The mind prospers with a lot of oxygen, and that is why yoga is a wonderful activity for teachers and students to perform every day. Clean air tends to clear the head and help you to focus. Every day you and your students should take a little break from what speaker Yvette Zgonc calls "the constipated curricula" in order to oxygenate your brains.

You need to try this: Stand up right now, open your mouth wide, and take a deep breath. Hold it for a few moments. Then, exhale slowly through your mouth. Proper yoga technique calls for exhaling through your nose, but this may be a very bad idea with young children.

Whenever you breathe with your students, try to focus their thoughts on happy, silly things. Here is an idea from a wonderful book called *It's All About Me: Personality Quizzes for You and Your Friends* (Phillips 2006). Let's determine where your confidence comes from.

Still standing, clasp your hands together. Which thumb is on top? Well, you may not know this, but you can tell a lot about yourself by which thumb is on top. If your left thumb is on top, you tend to rely on logic and reason. You are most confident when your decisions are based on real-world information. If your right thumb is on top, you tend to trust your intuition. You are most confident when your gut says you are doing the right thing. Facts, schmacts!

Look at your thumbs closely. Are they thin or thick? Well, you may not know this, but you can tell a lot about yourself by the thickness of your thumbs. If you think your thumbs are thin, you are most confident hanging with a few close friends. You like parties where everyone could fit on the same elevator. If you think your thumbs are thick, you are just as confident in large groups as one-on-one. You like parties where everyone can fit in the same stadium!

Now, would you say you have short thumbs or long thumbs? Well, you may not know this, but you can tell a lot about yourself by the length of your thumbs. If you think your thumbs are short, you work confidently and quickly. You are always the first person to finish a math test. If you think your thumbs are long, you work slowly and carefully. Yet you never seem to lose a thumb war. Go figure!

Sit down. Relax. Plop your hands on your lap, palm side down. Where does your left thumb land? Is it shaped like an "L," does it rest at a 45-degree angle, or is it touching your other fingers? Well, you may not know this, but you can tell a lot about yourself by where your left thumb rests. If it is like an "L," you are super-confident and like to be in charge. (Some people call you bossy. Have them fired.) If it is resting at a 45-degree angle, you are relatively confident. You care what people think about you, but not enough to actually change or do anything about it. Finally, if your left thumb is touching your fingers or under your palm, you might feel pretty unconfident now—like you want to hide from the world. But remember, you are thumb-one wonderful!

Breathe with your students as a way of breathing life back into your classroom. Both you and your students will appreciate the pause to regenerate your brains and your confidence.

⇒ Eat, Drink, and Be Merry

One thing to stress to students is that the little things, not the big things, matter most. Nothing relaxes people more than good meals together, so why not eat with your colleagues? If you are a principal, how about providing some refreshments at meetings? If you suffer from a condition known as "meeting narcolepsy," which means your mind typically falls asleep within the first five minutes of most meetings, perhaps it is a good idea to ask superiors to provide free coffee at meetings to maintain your focus.

Beginning teachers miss out on so much wisdom by avoiding veteran teachers. Do yourself a favor and ask one out to lunch. You can become a much better teacher through conversations with veterans. Yes, some may offer cynical views of education (it seems that when you have been in education for a long time, it is difficult not to develop these views), but they also offer a wealth of experience and knowledge about dealing with different situations. Following a presentation to a district in Mississippi, a teacher approached me and confessed that she was not as quick on her feet at answering questions as she would like to be, not realizing that my seemingly quick responses to new questions were really the result of dealing with similar questions hundreds of times before. I had learned this by eating lunch with veterans.

Wisdom is not confined to teachers. From time to time, buy coffee for a parent, a janitor, or the school secretary.

Simple gestures often create bonds that last a lifetime. Some of my best parent volunteers began the school year by simply dropping off their kids. It was through casual chats over coffee that their participation at school increased. Buy donuts, and share with everyone, including secretaries and janitors. Are these bribes? No, you are simply showing your colleagues, the staff, and the parents that you truly care about their thoughts and opinions. Food is a great way to bring people together.

Your most important job is to present students with a positive role model. Invite students to eat lunch with you in the classroom on occasion as a reward for good behavior (make sure it is a reward, as many teachers are so miserable that students do not want to be around them during mandated learning time, let alone during their lunch breaks). When rewarding students with lunch in the classroom, you'll find most seats filled with children eager to talk about things not scripted in the standardized schedule. The more you learn about your students, and the more they find out about you, the more you will trust one another.

So give it a try. Eat, drink, and be merry. You may be surprised at how much happier and more productive you become.

Maintain Balance

One definition of homeostasis is a state of psychological equilibrium obtained when tension or drive has been reduced or eliminated. It can be difficult for many teachers to relax in the current atmosphere of standards-based instruction that focuses all attention on testing. Point taken. Educators are all under a lot of stress. It is important, however, that educators keep things in perspective for themselves and—more importantly—for their students. As Little Orphan Annie so profoundly said, "The sun will come out tomorrow."

Too many teachers leave the profession because they get burned out. One outstanding teacher who had left his cushy, high-paying job as an accountant at a large firm to become an inner-city elementary school teacher once offered this bit of advice: Work will always be there, so keep it there. You could plan lessons every night until midnight, but you still will have more work to do. One of the best services you can do for your students is to take time for yourself.

Develop a hobby. Make friends with people who are not teachers. Talk about sports or needlepoint or foreign films—anything besides education. Keep your stress level down and you will be a better teacher.

Hydrate

Human bodies are estimated to be about 60–70 percent water. Your body needs water to regulate body temperature and to provide the means for nutrients to travel to all your organs. Water also transports oxygen to your cells, removes waste, and protects joints and organs. Blood is mostly water, and your muscles, lungs, and brain all contain a lot of water. According to every diet, drinking lots of water acts as an appetite suppressant. So, you need to be drinking lots of water as you teach. Drinking lots of water also keeps you more energetic, which is something you need all day, but especially in the afternoon.

You need to encourage your students to drink water throughout the day, as well. Also, remember to do your part for the environment, so ask students not to bring new bottles of water to class. Instead, have them bring water in a reusable water bottle. If you teach young children, show them how to fill the bottle halfway the night before school and put it in the freezer. When they wake up, they will find the water is frozen. They can fill the other half of the water bottle and—voila!—they now have ice water for the day. This is a pretty cool revelation to a first grader!

In high school, football coaches give water breaks as rewards after hard workouts. The problem is, many players have already keeled over from exhaustion! What if, instead, you choose to prevent students from keeling over by investing a little bit of time and common sense into hydrating? It will keep you and your students sharper and more alert throughout the day.

 Go to the Restroom

Here's an old joke for you:

How do teachers get through their days without using the restroom?

'Depends.

My first day of teaching presented me with numerous challenges. For one, I had no idea what half of the bells meant. I felt like a war veteran by the end of the day, hearing bells and ducking for cover to play things safe. Nobody had ever taken the time to tell me about restrooms, either. One of the most humiliating experiences of my life was walking into a boy's restroom on my first day of school where seven little boys were closely focused on my every move. It was quite a relief to discover that faculty members had their own restrooms.

Now that you have loaded up your students on a lot of water, you need to ensure that there are plenty of opportunities to use the restroom. Upon closer examination of world records, it is probably a safe bet that the people with the largest bladders in the world are teachers or tollbooth attendants. Contrary to many district policies, going to the restroom is not a waste of time. It is another way to get students up and moving. So, keep your students (and yourself) comfortable by integrating plenty of restroom breaks throughout the day. They do not need to take a long time, and the result will be better concentration on their seatwork and less on their "seat."

Seek Companionship

Several years ago, after a bad break-up, I fell into a deep depression that prompted me to isolate myself from the social scene for quite a while. Visiting my relatives, my aunt cheered me up when we walked by a middle-aged couple in the park holding hands and wearing matching T-shirts with matching chocolate ice cream stains. My aunt turned to me and said, "You see that, Danny. There's someone for everybody." I made it my business to start dating again.

If you are a teacher, you need to be cultivating relationships and fostering a love of learning—with everyone you meet. Society is in dire need of more educated people. The best way for teachers to help others is for them to first help themselves. Companionship is a basic physiological need, and indeed, having a supportive comrade can play a huge role in the success of many classrooms.

There are more than a few grumpy teachers who could benefit greatly from a bit of socialization. My students noticed how depressed I was after my girlfriend and I split. One of my students, Erica, misbehaved one day, and I asked her to go to "time-out" and write a reflection on how she could improve. Erica wrote: "I am so sory (sic) that I was bad, Mister Bercell (sic). I will be better. I love you. I would marry you." Isn't it remarkable how children have the ability to bring a smile to their teacher's face?

Having close friends and family, and making sure you foster and nurture those relationships, frees you up to focus on better ways to teach your students. If you are single, go out with your friends. If you are married, spend time with your spouse. And make sure you don't talk about teaching!

Nap

If you had to go to surgery and learned that your doctor had not slept in two days, how comfortable would you feel? Imagine flying with a pilot who had pulled four consecutive graveyard shifts. Do you think she would be at her best? Sleep matters!

One of the best practices in Spain is the siesta, the afternoon nap. People need their rest. Preschool and kindergarten teachers have the right idea, offering students time to nap every day, but the teachers should nap, as well.

Napping allows your mind and body to take a break. While many are under the false impression that naps are just for children or the elderly, naps can benefit people of all ages. The desire to nap is a trait shared by many mammals, and napping is still an important part of the day in many parts of the world. Plenty of great thinkers, including Thomas Edison and Albert Einstein, found naps to be an essential part of their creative thought process. Snoozing in the teacher's lounge for 15 minutes can be an enjoyable way to promote physical well-being, and naps have been known to improve people's moods and memories. Naps help rejuvenate, sharpen the senses and make a person more cheerful. Naps can help unleash the creative forces that surely made Edison and Einstein such strong proponents of the practice. If naps are good enough for them, they're good enough for everyone.

Snack

People like snacks. Many a heart races for desserts. How can you make your classroom as attractive as snacks and desserts?

There was once a woman who joined a weight-loss group and was dismayed to discover she had only lost a couple of pounds after dieting for a week. When her meeting leader asked her why she was upset after such a productive first week, the woman responded that her friend had lost 10 pounds in one week and assured her that she would, too. The disturbed leader inquired if the woman's friend was a doctor, and the woman shook her head. The leader asked the dieter if her friend was a nurse, and the woman shook her head again. "Well, is she a nutritionist?" the exasperated leader asked, and the woman said, "No, I think she's a liar!"

The brain loves food, and there are a variety of healthy snacks that can keep you focused. A good reason to share with students is to introduce them to healthier options like fruit, granola, and almonds, as opposed to the typical junk-food fare most of them prefer. The sooner schools can institute positive habits in their students, the greater positive effects teachers will see in the long run.

Doodle to Some Tunes

Even if not part of the standard curriculum, art and music should be integrated throughout the day, whether you are teaching kindergarteners or 12th graders.

Music feeds the soul, which is almost as important as feeding the belly. There are so many wonderful scenes in movies where a particular tune works magic between people. There is a scene in *The Breakfast Club* (1985) where bored high school students in detention hum the theme from *The Bridge on the River Kwai* (1957). After an argument with their lead singer, band members sulk in silence on the band's bus in *Almost Famous* (2000) while Elton John's "Tiny Dancer" plays on the radio. By the time the song ends, everyone on the bus is smiling and singing the lyrics together. Music has the remarkable ability to help form bonds, and it can even help students concentrate.

A study conducted by a researcher at Cambridge University (Andrade 2010) demonstrates the importance of drawing to the mind. According to the study, subjects given a doodling task while listening to a dull phone message had a 29 percent improved recall compared to their non-doodling counterparts. Although doodling may not work for all students, it could be helpful to some.

> "Daydreaming distracts (people) from (a) task, resulting in poorer performance," according to the study's author, Dr. Janet Andrade. "A simple task, like doodling, may be sufficient to stop daydreaming without affecting performance on the main task.... Doodling may be something we do because it helps to keep us on track with a boring task, rather than being an unnecessary distraction that we should try to resist doing."

Art and music are necessary "distractions" that help rather than inhibit students' thought processes. So turn on the tunes, and bring out the doodle pads!

 ## Eat Healthy Foods

A classroom is more dangerous than an emergency room when it comes to airborne diseases, so you need to take care of yourself. Take vitamins and eat healthier foods. Some essential foods for a healthy lifestyle include blueberries, nuts, salmon, broccoli, bananas, yogurt, olive oil, brown bread, spinach, and tomatoes.

A great strategy to stress to middle school students to help them retain information is to associate pieces of information with parts of their bodies. Try this mnemonic to remember these healthy foods.

Stand up. Start from head to toe, beginning with blueberries. Rub your scalp with both hands and say, "Blueberries on the brain." Now the way you are going to remember nuts is by tapping your shoulders and saying, "Nuts on the shoulders." After every new essential food is tied to a body part, it is important to repeat all the foods and body parts as a review: "Blueberries on the brain," (massage scalp), "nuts on the shoulders" (tap shoulders).

Now, wave your right hand like a wave in front of your heart, and say, "Salmon in the heart." Next, rub your tummy, and say, "Broccoli in the belly." Put your hands on your hips and say, "Bananas on the hips." Then put your hands on your gluteus and your maximus (your bottom) and say, "Two cups of yogurt!"

Are you blushing? Are you reviewing all the essential foods and movements after each new one? Now, continue. When thinking of olive oil, many people think "slick," so slide your hands down over your knees and say, "Olive oil!" Next, place your right hand on your right knee, and say, "Brown"; then place your left hand on your left knee and continue, "Bread." Afterward, stroke your shins, and say, "Spinach on the shins." (If you teach young children, point out that *spinach* and *shins* both have a short /i/ sound.) Finally, march in place, and shout, "Smashing tomatoes!"

Continue on in this manner, assigning a body part to each food. Don't be afraid to be goofy or include random gestures. These are entertaining and help aid memory.

Review all these steps, and you will remember the essential foods you need to eat to maintain a healthy lifestyle. Happy teachers are healthy teachers!

 Move Around

Stay still and school will eat you alive. You need to be constantly on the move! Wear a pedometer. The average elementary school teacher probably walks over 20,000 steps a day just in the classroom.

Speaker Harvey MacKay (1988) said, "I have known successful salespeople who were drunks, gamblers, liars, thieves…but I have never known a successful salesperson who sat on his [butt] all day." Teachers are in the sales profession. You sell learning every single day. When teachers brag that they managed to teach 20 standards in one day, that's worth a chuckle. How many of those standards do their students remember the following day, week, or month? If students do not remember it, the teacher taught them nothing. The brain loves movement, and one of the best ways to help students retain information is to get them up and moving. You are responsible for creating memories in your students. Students don't recall the scripted reading lesson, or which bullet point was the most meaningful to them. Yet they remember when they got up off their chairs and memorized essential healthy foods based on body part movements or when they learned about ants by taking a nature walk outside.

With today's active students (by the way—in the old days, students liked to move around, too), great teachers understand the importance of movement in stimulating the brain. Movement also inspires imagination, and it can lead to students and teachers enjoying themselves more in their limited time together.

 ## Hand Out Hugs A Plenty

Teachers are warned never to touch students. Well, if you teach young children, they are most definitely going to touch you, whether you want them to or not! No matter how many warnings you receive about teachers being sued for touching students, there are students who require a lot of extra attention and affection. I have heard it said that eight to ten touches a day help humans maintain emotional and physical health. In fact, many people cite a UCLA research study that confirmed the number, but I have never seen such a study so I question its validity.

Regardless, I like the idea: all of us prosper when we experience meaningful touches of affection. So, at the risk of being sued, hug your students. They will feel better, and so will you. If you cannot be so touchy, at the very least give lots of "high-fives," fist-bumps, and pats on the back. Show students how much they mean to you. Of course, you need to avoid being alone with students, and you need to always keep your door open.

There is a moving and horrifying story about a boy whose mother was an alcoholic. She neglected her children and became cruel and abusive when she was drunk. She beat this boy and forced him to live in a cold, dark, and filthy garage (yes, there are monsters out there). She treated her son like a slave and only fed him scraps after he performed chores. When the boy's second grade teacher tried to intervene on his behalf, the boy's mother punished him by changing his name to "It." She never called him anything else but "It," and she forbade her other children to call him by his name.

Teachers provided the only kindness this boy ever knew; they treated him with respect and compassion. At night, as he sat in that cold, dark garage, he pictured the faces of his teachers for comfort. Finally, when the boy was in fifth grade, a few courageous teachers, the principal, and the school nurse convinced officials at Social Services to step in and remove the abused boy from his home. That day, as the authorities came, the entire staff at the boy's school lined up to give him a hug, an impression that he would never forget. Before he left, this little fifth-grader made two solemn promises to his caring teachers: First, he vowed he would never forget them and their kindnesses to him; second, he decided he would do everything in his power to make them proud of him.

Twenty years later, that little boy, now a grown man, stood before his old teachers at Thomas Edison Elementary

School to thank them for what they did, and to fulfill his other promise. He gave those difference-makers a copy of his book, *A Child Called "It"* (1995). His name is Dave Pelzer, one of the only authors to have three books simultaneously on the *New York Times* bestseller list, and he has dedicated his life to helping other "youth at risk." And it all began with a hug.

You may not have a student who suffered such horrors as Dave Pelzer, but you certainly teach students who yearn for your affection. Why not invest in them?

Brew Coffee or Spray Air Freshener

Your classroom environment is critical to your own sanity and your students' learning. Great teachers create classroom environments that engage all of the senses. Keep this in mind.

Make your classroom visually appealing. Surround students with a lot of print and colors. It may not help them to concentrate with so much visual stimulation, but it certainly draws their interest. Consider the importance of accessibility to materials. When you teach young children, it is a good idea to wander around your room from time to time on your knees to ensure items are readily available to your students.

Place some natural air fresheners or brew some coffee in your classroom so that it does not smell like bodily fluids. You could even open a window. Allow your students to eat and drink in the classroom, especially when they read. Do you like to eat and drink while you read? One of the ways to promote students' lifelong love for reading is by facilitating sensory experiences that cause students always to associate reading and learning with fun and relaxation. Let your students listen to the music as they read. They may prefer to listen to hip-hop or pop music, at first. However, after a few weeks, students tend to inevitably begin to enjoy easier listening when they work: instrumental pieces like jazz, blues, classical, and nature sounds. Ask students to envision their ideal classroom, and then create it together. Happier students are more productive students. More productive students make our jobs easier and more rewarding.

Play Head Games

Psychology is fascinating. It is really amazing how people can manipulate others to believe certain things (and not just in negative ways). A smiling teacher dressed in bright colors with a warm classroom environment can convince students that they are going to achieve, the same way that Oprah Winfrey can get millions of people to feel that reading a certain book will change their lives.

If you're the teacher who "always gets stuck with the low kids," try a different tactic from day one. "You all need to help me," you can say to your students. "This is my first time teaching the gifted and talented students." There is a piece of ancient wisdom that says you should try to treat other people the way you want to be treated, and when you treat people like geniuses they start acting in that manner.

There are many great stories of football coaches who were experts at manipulating players. I will share three of my favorites. The first is personal. My high school football coach made us wear black shoes so we would appear slower on game films. While opposing coaches often added height and weight to their players to make them sound bigger and more intimidating, our coach listed us as shorter and lighter in the programs so opposing teams were startled by our sizes on game day. The lesson? You can turn negatives into surprising positives.

The next story is about Knute Rockne, legendary coach of several national champion Notre Dame teams. He constantly used manipulation to his team's advantage. Once, when Notre Dame faced a critical game against a vastly superior Southern California team (USC), Rockne recruited every brawny student he could find at Notre Dame and suited them up in the school football uniform. On the day of the game, the Southern California team ran out on the field first and awaited the visiting Fighting Irish. Then, out of the dressing room came an army of green giants who kept on coming and coming. The USC team panicked. While USC's coach reminded his players that Notre Dame could only play 11 men at a time, the damage was already done—USC lost by being intimidated by the Irish size. The lesson? People will believe what they see. Build a team mentality in your classroom, and present a united front when facing obstacles. You'll be surprised how quickly the obstacles can be overcome.

Finally, NFL Hall of Fame quarterback Joe Montana describes how he walked by his San Francisco 49er coach Bill Walsh before their first Super Bowl appearance. As Walsh lay on his back, seemingly ignorant of Montana's presence, Montana heard Walsh mumbling about how much trouble Montana was going to have throwing against Cincinnati's defense. Montana walked away determined to prove him wrong. When sharing the story with teammate Ronnie Lott after the game, Lott confessed that he, too, had walked by Walsh and overheard Walsh mumbling about what a challenge Lott would face against a much stronger Cincinnati offense. The lesson? Motivation comes in many forms. Challenge your students to do their best despite what anyone thinks of them.

Many great teachers constantly point out how they would be lost without assistance from their students. One example was a teacher who was a master at highlighting each student's strength. If Manuel was excellent at short division, this teacher would refer every student with a short division question to Manuel—the "class expert." All the students in this class recognized that they had strengths and were anxious to demonstrate those strengths to others.

Good teachers are good coaches. They get in their students' heads by manipulating them to think that success is inevitable.

⟫ Be a Thermostat, Not a Thermometer

Medical missionary David Livingstone (of the legendary question, "Dr. Livingstone, I presume?") spent most of his adult life living in primitive conditions in Africa in the 19th century. While exploring in Africa, Dr. Livingstone received a letter from some friends with good intentions. "We would like to send other men to you," the letter read. "Have you found a good road into your area yet?" Dr. Livingstone responded promptly. "If you have men who will only come if they know there is a good road, I don't want them. I want strong and courageous men who will come if there is no road at all."

It is a misconception that anyone can teach. It takes a lot of hard work to be a great teacher. Even if only one teacher blindly follows a mandated program that follows a dull script, that is enough to discourage students from loving learning. Too many teachers do as they are told and never question why they do things that way. These teachers are "thermometers;" they simply tell the temperature in their rooms. Any good administrator worth his or her weight will recognize that the best teachers may use unorthodox approaches, but serve as thermostats, setting high expectations and accepting no less than excellence from all students.

Great reading teachers read wonderful books aloud to students and provide them with plenty of books that they can read on their own for fun. The best math teachers engage students by posing interesting problems and encouraging students to think of multiple solutions. Teachers who leave a lasting legacy constantly impact students by going above and beyond the minimum that is required of them.

Society needs teachers who are thermostats. Thermostats set the temperature. Be a thermostat. You set the climate of your classroom. Do not let somebody else set your climate for you.

Reflection Questions

1. The best teachers manage to get their students to believe in themselves. What are you doing in your class to help students believe in themselves?

2. Are you in control, or do you let others tell you what to do in your classroom? What kind of example are you to your students? Do you expect students to do what you tell them to, or do you challenge them to think critically?

3. What are some ways you are supporting the physiological needs of your students? How are you taking care of your own physiological needs?

Safety Needs

Overview

Once people satisfy their basic physiological needs, Maslow argues that their safety needs take precedence and tend to dominate their behavior. These needs revolve around security and stability.

How can teachers create classrooms that offer students secure and stable environments? According to Marian Diamond, a professor in the Department of Integrative Biology at the University of California, Berkeley (Diamond and Hopson 1998), an enriched environment for children:

- includes a steady source of positive support.

- stimulates all of the senses (though not all at once).

- has an atmosphere free of undue pressure and stress but is suffused with a degree of pleasurable intensity.

- presents a series of novel challenges that are neither too easy nor too difficult for the child at his or her stage of development.

- allows social interaction for a significant percentage of activities.

- promotes the development of a broad range of skills and interests: mental, physical, aesthetic, social, and emotional.

- gives the child an opportunity to choose many of his or her efforts and to modify them.

- provides an enjoyable atmosphere that promotes exploration and the fun of learning.

- allows the child to be an active participant rather than a passive observer.

Best-selling author Malcolm Gladwell tells a delightful story about Howard Moskowitz (Gladwell 2008). Moskowitz is a well-known experimental psychologist in the field of psychophysics and an inventor of world-class market research technology. Working for Pepsi® in the 1970s, Moskowitz was charged with finding the perfect formula for Diet Pepsi®. His data bedeviled him for years before he realized that Pepsi® should not have been looking for the perfect Diet Pepsi®—they should have been looking for the perfect Diet Pepsis®.

Moskowitz's research with various food products illuminated the public's different tastes. In essence, the perfect Diet Pepsi® or Vlasic® pickle or Prego® tomato sauce for one person can be very different for another person. By the mid-1980s, Howard Moskowitz changed the landscape of the food industry forever by insisting manufacturers think differently. He discovered that there are no perfect or imperfect products, only different kinds of products that suit different kinds of people. Moskowitz helped promote the notion that universal principles are a myth, and variability in taste should always be considered. Because of Moskowitz, grocery stores today carry seven different kinds of vinegar, 14 different kinds of mustard, and 71 different kinds of olive oil.

The lesson learned is that teachers should embrace diversity and strive to create highly differentiated environments that acknowledge individuals' varying interests and needs. The same is true for teachers. Some bring lots of goofy energy to class, while others find their rhythm with highly predictable routines.

Students feel safe when their individual needs are met. They feel secure, respected, and valued when consideration has been given to their individual preferences. So, what does a safe and secure learning environment look like? This chapter offers the principles inherent in creating a safe and nurturing learning environment.

Quick Strategies for Creating a Safe and Secure Physical Classroom Environment

1. **Give choices.** Provide many choices in your classroom. Depending on your students, they could be offered choices in the books that they read, the students with whom they sit, or the types of activities which they complete during instruction.

2. **Divide and conquer.** Designate different areas of the classroom for different subject areas (e.g., mathematics centers, social studies centers, science centers). Secondary teachers can designate different areas of the classroom for different projects.

3. **Inspire artistry.** Provide a variety of writing materials (realizing that some students who show little interest in writing with a pencil will jump at the chance to use a marker or crayon). Offer clay, cameras, and other materials that can attract the artistic instincts of your diverse students.

4. **Activate the sense of touch.** Supply a variety of tactile objects for instructional purposes. Bean counters and pennies make cheap, easy mathematics manipulatives; stuffed animals are great reading companions. Additionally, many teachers offer small, soft items like racquet balls, hair scrunchies, and stress balls for students to hold as a way to boost concentration skills.

5. **Offer praise and descriptive feedback.** Celebrate students' growth by posting examples of all students' work throughout the classroom. (Make sure to ask students' permission to post their work, in case some may not desire such public displays.)

6. **Soothe the soul with music.** Play different types of music throughout the day (e.g., play soothing jazz or classical music while students write, and hip-hop or classic rock while cleaning the classroom).

7. **Establish a print-rich environment.** Label items throughout the classroom, and post labels in multiple languages (e.g., label items in English, Spanish, and Japanese or any other language that is represented in your room). The classroom ceiling can be filled with posters of song lyrics and poems, so even daydreamers are inundated with print.

8. **Brighten up.** Consider the colors throughout your classroom and how they affect students' learning (e.g., some colors may be bright and stimulating, while others may soothe students).

9. **Declutter.** Maintain plenty of space throughout the classroom so that students do not feel restricted. If your classroom feels like the economy class section of an airplane, you need to create more space.

10. **Keep it comfortable.** Offer cozy, inviting furniture (e.g., cushions and rocking chairs).

Fifteen Ways to Meet Your Safety Needs

 Do It Your Way

A pastor once told a story about a Sunday school class of first graders talking about heaven. A little girl, who was a bit of a know-it-all, coolly informed her classmates that "if you are good, you get to go to heaven." When a boy in the class asked what happens if you are bad, the little girl replied, "Then you go to the principal's office."

You are probably an open-minded individual, willing to try new strategies in your classroom. But remember, the true joy of teaching comes when you find the method that works best for you. Conforming to others' methods erodes your passion in your classroom. All it takes is a few bad experiences for you to vow never to go down that path again. Some years ago when the federal government faced imminent shutdown if Congress did not pass the President's budget, there was a lively debate in the Senate. Representing the Republican point of view, Senator Bob Dole of Kansas said, "The latest budget not only asks Republicans to hang themselves, but now (the Democrats) want (Republicans) to supply the rope. If you want to hang me, you supply the rope." The speech gave me a good chuckle, and I realized that is a good philosophy of life.

Teaching style is very overrated. Some teachers instill a passion for learning in their students by bouncing off the walls, while others are as calm as a placid lake. Superior teachers find their comfort zone and incorporate their passion every day. If you're not funny, don't tell jokes. Teachers need to understand that if they love quilting and base their lessons around their passion, students will feel that passion. From passion comes joy, and this joy is contagious.

Do not live life with regrets. The world will always need good teachers. Doing it somebody else's way—if it is something you do not believe in—is a slow way to die. Think of the old Frank Sinatra song, and do it your way. One of my greatest mentors used to tell me that she had been teaching for over 40 years, and in that time the district had introduced over 35 different reading programs. "I have one. Mine," she said. "And it works." Mrs. Turner was strong in her beliefs (a little too strong in the eyes of some of her superiors), but there was one thing nobody could ever question about her: She was a darn good teacher. She had a very concrete belief system, she loved what she did, and she produced remarkable results.

It can be tricky in this current assessment-driven educational environment, but you need to follow your heart *and* mind in your classroom. Adapt to the individual needs of your students, who vary by year, class period, and desk. If your district-mandated core curriculum is not serving their needs, say something, or better yet, do something about it. Join the district textbook adoption committee, and find good supplemental resources. Rally some supporters and be the change you want to see in your classroom.

 ## Become a Teacher Leader

I was so annoyed that union dues were automatically taken out of my check that I became the union representative for my school. Whatever your opinion of teacher unions, they hold tremendous political influence. In fact, the California Teachers Association spent more money than any other lobbying group over the last decade to influence voters and officials (McGreevy 2010). While they may cause more problems than they solve, unions do offer benefits.

It is for this reason young teachers should consider becoming union representatives for their school sites. Every teacher has a problem, and the person he or she is most likely to turn to is the school's union rep. As a representative, you will become acquainted with all of your colleagues, and they will get to know you. One of the best ways to improve, as a teacher, is to watch a lot of teachers. My own teaching benefited immensely from conversations I had with colleagues about various strategies. Many of these conversations begin when a colleague has a question for the union representative.

My own union experiences taught me that unions are not to be feared. Their legal services, for example, are a tremendous resource for teachers. The time commitment is reasonable, and every encounter is an opportunity to learn how to enhance your teaching. In many cases, I learned about things I should never do as a teacher. But most importantly, I forged relationships in my union encounters with scores of teachers I probably would never have met otherwise.

My experience with unions is the foundation for one of my guiding principles. You need to try to take things that you may perceive as negatives and turn them into positives. This Pollyanna approach can lead you to be healthier, happier, and wiser.

There are two types of teachers: excuse makers and problem solvers (a.k.a. Friday teachers and Monday teachers). True teacher leaders solve problems.

The excuse makers like to hang out in the teachers' lounge or limp through the hallways, whining and griping to anyone within earshot. They always get "the bad kids," and they always seem to get the short end of the stick, if you listen to them. These are the "Friday teachers" who cannot wait for the weekend or the summer break or retirement. To hear them tell it, teaching is about as appealing as filling out a tax form.

Surround yourself with problem solvers. Be a problem solver. Students need "Monday teachers." These are the teachers who cannot wait for Monday morning when they can try a new lesson plan, create a new bulletin board, or practice a new game with their students. To these teachers, every day brings new challenges that keep teaching exciting and exhilarating. These are the folks that attend professional development workshops after 30 years in the classroom in hopes of still improving. Complacency is a killer, and these teachers are always on the cutting edge.

Lead at your school. Leaders mentor new teachers. Some toil as their school site's union representative. Others lead with kindness by dropping nice notes in their colleagues' mailboxes, buying flowers for the PTA president, treating for breakfast, and sharing extra resources with colleagues. A positive approach is the foundation of a healthier and happier work environment.

Meet and Greet

Start your day off with love and joy. Greet students at your classroom door and give them high-fives. You can squat by your classroom door and greet students individually by name and ask them if they are going to have a great day. They inevitably yell, "Yes!" and then they are off and running.

Did you ever watch *The Andy Griffith Show* (1960–1968)? One thing to appreciate about small towns is the simple hospitality of neighbors. Bankers may lend money based on a handshake, waitresses know everyone's name and tipping pattern, and the newspaper writes about every person in town at least once a year. One of the best ways to promote school unity and prosperity is to make a point of getting to know everybody.

As a great example of a mentor, "Ethel" was a teacher and administrator in Compton, California, for over 40 years. You have never met a kinder, sharper educator. Ethel taught me the value of using sugar instead of vinegar to solve problems. She was a gentle woman who walked gingerly but with purpose. No matter which school she visited, Ethel inevitably knew every teacher, janitor, administrator, and secretary. If she did not know somebody, she headed straight for that person with her hand extended and a kind greeting. Everybody loved Ethel because she took the time to greet everyone and get to know a little something about each person. She took pleasure in hearing all about people, and they took pleasure in telling Ethel all that was going on in their lives. Ethel was so effective because of her genuine interest in seeing people succeed. As a result, people tried harder when they were around her. Let her model inspire you to get to know all of the people you work with—from teaching colleagues to the cafeteria workers to the crossing guards.

Enclose Students in the Circle of Life

One of the best things to do with your students every day is to sing. Sing all of the time in all of your classes. With your youngest students, begin the day in a singing circle. (We called ours the "Circle of Life" after the popular song from Disney's® *The Lion King* [1994].)

While singing with students, scan your class in search of students who look like they have not had enough sleep, who wore the same clothes from the previous day or who appear to be in a grumpy mood. Afterwards, take those students aside and check to make sure everything is all right. Have pillows ready in your reading corner, so that sleepy children can take a short nap before you try to teach them anything. Keep a lot of apples and graham crackers in your desk for students who missed breakfast. Yes, you probably could notice these things by circulating among the class during your opening lessons, but preventive medicine is best. Singing as a group gives you an excellent opportunity to diagnose any possible difficulties before the day begins, and the simple act of singing together calms a lot of tensions before they have a chance to explode.

Some folks believe singing is just for little kids. Honestly, you may sing more often with older students than younger ones; middle school and high school students take themselves too seriously and need the singing to loosen up. I've had students complain, "Man, this is stupid! I hate these songs! You wore that jacket yesterday!" Then, if we don't sing as a class, these same students will complain, "Hey, when are we singing?"

Students need to be up and moving. Singing clears the mind and frees the soul. There is strength in numbers. A lot of shy students or English language learners who say very little at the beginning of the year soon confidently join in. Hold hands, swing your arms and sing at various volumes. Singing at the start of the day allows students to get out any extra energy that might prevent them from concentrating during opening lessons. Sometimes, it is just important to act a little goofy to start your day. Make up tunes or use common tunes, but chanting together works just fine, too. Some songs from my regular repertoire are shown on the following pages.

"Days of the Week" (English)
Sunday

Monday

Tuesday

Wednesday

Thursday

Friday

Saturday—

(*clap*)

The days of the week!

"Días de la Semana" (Spanish)
domingo

lunes

martes

miércoles

jueves

viernes

sábado—

(*clap*)

¡Los días de la semana!

"Ugh Ugh Uga Ug" (Gibberish)

ugh

ooo

aya

ugha

uya

egga

urra—

(*clap*)

ugh ugh uga ug

"Morning Routine"

I wake up in the morning—and make my bed.

I step into the shower—and wash my head.

I brush my teeth—and comb my hair.

I fix a big breakfast—and eat all that is there.

I dress myself—and walk to school.

I come ready to learn—and that's why I'm cool.

Some of these songs use "gibberish," which is a language all children seem to understand, much to the frustration of adults. Think about all the gibberish you hear during yard duty. Typically, only one or two teachers supervise students on the playground during recess. You will inevitably be approached by children with skinned knees wailing, "Maaa—estro...me...due—le...my...knee." You may be inclined to say, "Please tell me in English or Spanish. I do not understand gibberish." (Eventually you will be conversant in all three languages!)

Start with a Morning Meeting

One of the first things to know as a beginning teacher is to train students how to facilitate strong morning meetings. Basically, during the first month of school, show students how to run the class, and then for the rest of the year, let them run it. Stay on the sidelines as much as possible. Students tend to forget things that their teacher tells them, but they remember everything they learn from each other.

Ideally, the entire day could follow a morning meeting format (Brassell 2009). Even if you teach kindergartners, those children can take control of the classroom. In Japan, elementary students serve lunch and clean their school. They learn responsibility at a young age—something educators seem to have lost touch with in the United States. Any child is capable of anything when given a little trust and guidance.

Elementary students can run morning meetings like a news broadcast. Choose an "anchor person" to run the broadcast and describe duties of various students. Student roles can include a "weather person" who describes the weather conditions, a "sportscaster" who describes various games and activities in which the class will participate on that day, and an "entertainment correspondent" who leads the class in various songs and poetry recitations. The morning meeting broadcast can also feature reporters who may report on student progress in different curricular areas, inform the class of important events like birthdays, and share tidbits from their personal lives.

Since most middle school teachers only have about 50 minutes in a class period, they need to be more economical with their time. Allow three different students each day to share news. Or, have one read aloud an important item from that date in history, while another reads a current news story item, and a third reads an item called "news of the weird." Provide a brief science article for one student to read at the beginning of class, while another keeps track of student homework, another student checks attendance, and one more passes around a bucket for students to post questions they have regarding the previous night's homework.

Regardless of the grade being taught, morning meetings in one form or another can fill the class with noise and laughter and start class in a very positive, productive way. Students take their roles seriously, whether they are leading the meeting as the "anchor person" or delivering the "weather and plants" report. Some students have to practice their roles for days (for example, students who read brief biographies on a famous person's birthday or discuss a poem of the day), while others become comfortable off-the-cuff with their classmates (such as students who share something from home). What is important is that all students participate, and everyone has fun. The more your students laugh and play, the happier they are. When students are happy, that is when they learn.

Introduce Mrs. Fields

Students need to feel safe in the classroom. Probably one of the biggest pet peeves of any teacher is tattling. Kids love to rat each other out. They have no qualms about getting each other into trouble, and many teachers find themselves constantly irritated by students who tattle. Your joy is inversely affected by the number of irritating interactions you have with students, colleagues, administrators, and parents. So, you need to figure out a way to put an end to tattling—at least in your presence.

There are usually only three reasons why children tattle. First, they want attention. Second, they want to get their buddy in trouble. Third, someone is in danger. In truth, students really just want to get their complaints off their chests. Yes, kids are like most adults. They really just want to gripe. I taped a poster of an elderly woman on a wall, and the students and I named her Mrs. Fields (because the kids love Mrs. Fields' cookies). Then, whenever a student approached me to tattle, I informed him or her that I did not have time to listen to any complaints, and I advised that student to go tell Mrs. Fields. Students wandered over to the poster and voiced their concerns to Mrs. Fields. One day I noticed one of my boys, Carlos, had been talking to Mrs. Fields for quite some time. "Is everything okay?" I asked. Carlos nodded and said, "Yeah, Mrs. Fields is taking care of it."

 ## Think and Grow Rich

We all know that there is not much money in teaching. There is concern that great teachers are leaving the profession because they cannot pay their bills. Here are a few financial tips.

As of 2009, The U.S. Federal Government offers a $1,500 tax credit to teachers for supplies which they purchase for their classrooms. When your good accountant prepares your long tax form, make sure he or she checks that credit for you. (**Note:** Hire a good accountant and file a long form, because you will save a lot of time, stress, and money by doing both. A good accountant should be able to get a refund for any teacher. Make sure you keep your receipts.)

Once you have spent $1,500 on your classroom, stop. That is money out of your pocket, and it will stress you out and give you something to gripe about in the teacher's lounge. Being creative about how you spend that $1,500 is critical. It is even more important to creatively not spend money on your classroom. Especially in impoverished schools, where there are not enough teaching supplies or other materials for students. Turn the lack of resources into teachable moments by showing students how to take items at your disposal and utilize them for different uses. Think of yourself as a cross between *MacGyver* (1985) and *The A-Team* (1983). Use milk crates for bookshelves, milk cartons for planters, coffee cans as supply holders, and construction paper as incentives. It does not take much to excite a young child.

Finally, maximize your retirement. Teachers can participate in what are called 403(b) plans, the education version of a 401(k). Speak to a financial consultant, as you want to talk to an expert about this. There are significant benefits to planning early for your retirement. Know that if you placed $1,000 per month into your retirement account, the actual amount of money taken out of your paycheck would be less because it would not be taxed. Again, there are highly qualified people who can advise you on financial matters, and it is important to your own happiness that you seriously consider your retirement sooner rather than later. Financial distress is one of the top reasons for divorces in this country, and it also contributes significantly to teachers leaving the classroom.

Since this is a book about joy, here is another encouraging story about my friend and mentor, Mrs. Turner.

Mrs. Turner taught in Compton, California. Compton has battled a multitude of problems in its history. But Compton is home to Mrs. Turner, and when she noticed drug dealers renting a home on her street, she took her savings, purchased the home, and rented it to a nice family from her church. She earned enough money from that home to purchase another run down home on her block, and rented that to another nice family. Pretty soon Mrs. Turner was a minor real estate mogul. Mrs. Turner made a difference every day in the lives of her students, and every evening she returned to a neighborhood she single-handedly transformed from a drug-ridden slum to a tree-lined street filled with young, church-going families. Yes, there are angels among us, and many of them are in classrooms.

Be Proud and Say It Loud

Say it loud: "I am a teacher, and I am proud!" Do not let people belittle your profession. If you think you have a dead-end job, get a different one. Your world is what you believe it to be. Kids deserve someone who loves what he or she does. Kids will inherit your attitude. If you do not love teaching, there is very little reason for you to be in the profession.

A lot of people are ashamed to be teachers. The famous Greek philosopher "Anonymous" once said, "Those who can, do. Those who can't, teach." To which Woody Allen replied, "Those who can't teach, teach gym." There are a lot of great teachers out there, and it is highly unlikely that any of them do not love teaching. What makes them great is that while they may be burdened with pay cuts, work furloughs, scripted programs, and endless standardized tests, they still admit that they love working with children. They love to see the light bulb go on in a student's head. They still get a kick out of the transformations that they see in their students.

When you go to parties and tell people that you are a teacher, do you get one of these two annoying responses? The first is, people will start asking random questions about state capitals, the subjunctive tense, and integers. Tell them, "I'm a teacher, not Google™." (Why some people expect teachers to be know-it-alls is beyond me.) The second response is akin to the reaction that they might have if you told them that you had a fatal disease. The moment that they discover that you work in education, people look at you with pity in their eyes. You know how to respond? Stand up, and say it loud: "I am a teacher, and I am proud!"

Surround Yourself with Positives

Negative energy will suck the life right out of you. You need to surround yourself with positive energy. Remember Pink Floyd's, "The Wall"? That's the song that says, "We don't need no education." Don't get freaked out, but do tune your radio to a more uplifting station.

Inspiring teachers is imperative because we need to motivate future teachers to work at many of our difficult-to-staff classrooms in the inner city. My advice? Stay away from negative faculty meetings. Why? They are filled with negative energy. Do you find yourself keeping quiet at meetings? Is it because your ideas are ridiculed or completely ignored? Contrast that with the experience of working at a charitable foundation called BookEnds.

BookEnds is a charity created by an eight-year-old boy that provides classroom libraries in underresourced areas. At every meeting, board members go out of their way to praise the insights of their colleagues. Even if an idea is silly, the board members understand that encouraging participation often leads them to have innovative ideas of their own. In turn, colleagues encourage each other. The result is a board that guided a tiny nonprofit into a burgeoning organization. To date, BookEnds has donated over two million books to over 530 schools, detention centers, and rehabilitation facilities, and enlisted over a quarter of a million student volunteers. Positive energy produces more positive energy, leading to positive results.

Would you like to know the secret to a long life? Turn off the negative television news on occasion, and read a funny children's book. The bad news tonight is the same as it was 100 years ago: The world is coming to an end, and the President is doing a bad job. Use the time you once spent in front of the television set to read a wonderful children's book. You will impress your friends when you can say you read a book cover to cover in one evening.

Have you ever heard anybody complain joyfully? Surround yourself with happy people and happy thoughts. That is one of the reasons to read a lot of funny books to students. Kids have the rest of their lives to experience sadness, tragedy, and misery; why not get them laughing in your class? I judge my own presentations by how much my audience laughs. Stay positive and surround yourself with positive people. Your attitude will be that of the company you keep and the books you read.

Attend Good Professional Development Events

A little boy used to go to church with his grandparents every Sunday morning. His grandmother sat in the choir and had to endure the murmurs of her friends when the boy's grandfather nodded off to sleep in the middle of the preacher's sermon every Sunday. Exasperated, Grandma offered to pay the little boy 50 cents to poke Grandpa in the ribs when he was caught napping.

The plan worked perfectly for several months, until Easter Sunday. The church was overflowing, and Grandma took her place alongside her friends in the choir. She saw her husband begin to nod off, but her grandson made no effort to wake him. She shot him a couple of insistent glares, but her grandson did not move. Grandpa even began snoring loudly during the service, much to the embarrassment of Grandma, and still her grandson failed to poke Grandpa. Grandma was most displeased after the service, and she confronted her grandson. "Why didn't you poke Grandpa in the ribs like I told you?" she asked. "You knew I would pay you 50 cents to keep your grandfather awake." The little boy shrugged. "I know, Grandma," he said. "But Grandpa gave me a dollar to let him sleep."

Have you ever heard the expression, "You get what you pay for?" Have you ever wondered why many school district trainings are lousy? Have you ever had to sit through a school training given by a poorly prepared trainer, someone who has never taught in the classroom (or knows nothing about how to give an engaging presentation, for that matter)? Isn't it ironic that a lot of the teaching "experts" who encourage teachers to facilitate lots of interaction with students hardly permit interaction during their presentations?

Beware of ineffective professional development. Look for titles like "75 Reading Strategies in 75 Minutes," or "50 Terrific Differentiated Instruction Tricks." *PowerPoint*™ presentations filled with indecipherable quotes that fill an entire page, preceded by slides with endless bullet points, are another sign of poor professional development. If the presenter spends the first 10 minutes telling you why he or she is qualified to speak to you, he or she is probably not qualified to speak to you. The best professional development trainings provide materials that teachers can use immediately in their classrooms. Teachers should feel good about themselves and their professions after attending a good training.

Talk with your administrator and ask him or her to pay for you to attend a good conference from time to time with legitimate, professional speakers. If you attend a professional development training that was not worthwhile, you should inform your administrator so he or she does not rehire that trainer. Good professional development speakers can inspire teachers. Teachers do not just want a paycheck; they need to feel like they are valued and appreciated.

Distinguish Rights from Privileges

A lot of joy left the teaching profession when lawsuits about abuse broke down the trust between teachers and students. Clearly, any teacher who physically or sexually abuses a child in any way should be removed from the profession. Mentally abusing students is unacceptable, as well. No teacher should ever put up with such abuse, either. Students and teachers have a right to a safe learning environment. However, political correctness has often run amok. As a result, many teachers are scared to discipline students because they do not want to risk getting sued. It is important then, in this day and age, for teachers to become knowledgeable about their legal rights, as well.

Classroom management is one of the most pressing challenges for beginning teachers. What is the best classroom management plan? Here's a gem that any good teacher already knows: Make your class so engaging that the biggest punishment you can issue a student is to not allow them to participate with the rest of the class. Too often, the entire class suffers consequences for one or two students' negative behavior. This is not fair at all.

One of the first talks to have with students is about the difference between a right and a privilege. For example, "You have a right to eat lunch," you may tell students, "but it is a privilege that I allow you to eat lunch with your friends." Students start to turn their heads, crinkle their noses and raise an eyebrow. "You have a right to use the restroom," you may continue, "but it is a privilege if I allow you to use it six times a day without a doctor's note." Teachers cannot take away student's rights, but they can take away their privileges. You will succeed as a class when everyone learns to "play ball."

Additionally, point out that while you can take away privileges, you may also grant privileges. The most important time in class is free-reading time, which should take place in at least three 10-minute chunks throughout the day in an elementary classroom. (Middle-school and high school teachers can provide time at the beginning and end of each period.) At the beginning of the year, allow students to brainstorm privileges that they would like while reading (e.g., listening to music, eating, reading with friends, or reading under desks). For each day that everyone reads successfully, grant an additional privilege. Students can learn from a very early age that hard work pays off.

 ## Stand Up for Your Peeps

Ecologists at the University of Washington were astonished to discover that willow trees transmit a warning to other willows about impending danger from as far away as 200 feet. When caterpillars attack, the willow trees emit a chemical signal that travels with the wind. This "distress signal" alerts distant trees to prepare their protection—phenol in the leaves—which caterpillars find to be distasteful. The individual trees have the ability to behave in a way that benefits not just themselves, but the whole species.

Stress the importance of kindness to your students. Model it every day. Children should be kind to others and stand up for their friends. There is no better book to illustrate this point than Kathryn Otoshi's *One* (2008), a picture book that cleverly teaches about bullying—as well as numbers and colors. It is a deceptively simple book that can teach leaders in education and business about the importance of team building.

Your classroom, your school, your district—these are your families. You may have disagreements in your families, but heaven help you if some "interloper" says anything bad about any of them in front of you.

Are you proud of where you teach? Are the students, parents, teachers, and administrators in your school and district near and dear to your heart? Remember, you are all on the same team, and teams with shared goals, passion, and determination are nearly unstoppable. If you truly love what you do, you need to stand up for all of the people around you. That is how leaders are made.

Show Up

Students depend on their teachers. Your job is to be there every day. If you want near-perfect attendance, you need to demonstrate near-perfect attendance. Woody Allen once said, "Eighty percent of success is showing up."

Many kindergartners go to bed with their backpacks already strapped on, but many eighth graders go to bed thinking of ways to get sick. What happened in those eight years? If teachers are doing their jobs well, their students should be banging on their classroom doors at 6:00 A.M. because they are so excited for school to start.

Do you know a teacher who takes every sick day and volunteers to be on any potential jury? This is a person who should not be teaching. Other teachers make sure that they are at school no matter what because nothing is more important to them than their students. Don't risk your health or the health of your students, but consider: what kind of teacher are you?

Talk It Out

During a mathematics exercise one day in class, a student blurted out that his father had been shot that weekend. How does a teacher respond to this kind of news? Should you nod and say, "That's too bad, now let's try to focus on numerators and denominators"? Or, do you decide to take the opportunity to talk about the situation with the student? There is power in discussion.

Discussing sensitive topics is sensitive business, so tread gently. Literature is a great teaching tool, as a book has been written about just about any type of issue a student could be having. There are books about bullying, not speaking English as a first language, and bed-wetting. Whenever an individual student has a problem that needs discussing, try to deal with the issue without mentioning the student in question. Whatever the issue though, teachers need to stress kindness, respect, and understanding, as everyone has something to deal with eventually. A classroom is supposed to function as a team where "everyone has each other's backs."

Henry Kissinger relates a story about when he was a boy growing up in Bavaria in the 1930s. One of the bullies of his neighborhood once caught up to him and began giving him a hard time. Instead of fighting—which would only end in Kissinger's defeat—he talked his way out of the situation. Nobody was hurt, and Kissinger discovered he had a gift for talking things out. Thank goodness, since Kissinger later emigrated to the United States, became secretary of state, and helped broker peace in many areas of the world—all through talking. His words achieved unity.

When everyone agrees on the things needed, teachers can build unity in their classrooms. One may not always get all the things he or she wants, but his or her needs are met. Model for students the power of working problems out through kind words rather than through brute force and insults. Communication is the key, and learning the power of listening is something from which almost everyone can benefit. Former South African president and Nobel laureate Nelson Mandela said that he has always made it a point to listen to everyone's point of view before offering his own. Mandela calls this "leading from behind." The truly great teachers have a habit of listening to students' opinions and acknowledging them.

Give People Space

When class-size reduction was passed in California, a lot of schools had to find classroom space. Some simply put curtains or paper-thin cubicle walls inside existing classrooms and voilà—two classrooms in one! That is not ideal for children. As funding for this program declines, classrooms will house more students than ever. A fire marshal once barged in my classroom and reprimanded me for hanging students' artwork from my lights. "That's a fire hazard," he scolded me. I pointed out to him that I had over 40 kids in a classroom built for 20, and I asked him if that was a fire hazard. "Tell you what," I said "I'll remove the artwork when you remove the extra students."

Students need to get up and move. Even if you have limited space in your classroom, your job is to give students the illusion of space. Let children spread out when they read. Provide centers or workstations throughout the room for students to go for refuge. When run properly, centers and workstations provide a stable opportunity for students to reinforce concepts together. If nothing else, open up your door and take the students outside your classroom.

Reflection Questions

1. What are some ways you create a positive and welcoming physical environment in your classroom?

2. Are there negative influences in your life that are keeping you from bringing joy to the classroom? What can you do to minimize those influences, or at least keep them from impacting your attitude in the classroom?

3. Do your students feel safe in the classroom? How can you tell? How are you offering students safe ways to communicate their fears and insecurities?

Love and Belonging Needs

Overview

After physiological and safety needs are met, the third layer of needs Maslow identifies is social, involving feelings of belonging. Everyone needs to feel a sense of belonging and acceptance, whether it comes from larger cultural or heritage connections, a professional sports team, or a smaller group like family or classmates. Everyone needs to love and feel loved by others. You need to feel like you belong.

In the movie *Grease* (1978), Danny (played by John Travolta) decides that he needs to become a jock to impress Sandy (played by Olivia Newton-John). He seeks the help of the high school coach (played by Sid Caesar). Danny tries his hand at football, basketball, and baseball, all to hilarious results, before finding his sport—track. Finally, Danny feels like he belongs.

What is your "sport"? Do you have strengths and weaknesses that differ from your colleagues? It is every teacher's responsibility to determine the individual needs of each student in his or her class. Teachers' and students' joy comes from their uniqueness. Differentiated instruction begins with assessing a student's readiness or abilities. Teachers need to determine each student's proficiency, which may be in a constant state of fluctuation. Good teachers play off the strengths of their students.

Ken Robinson (2009) tells a wonderful story of Gillian Lynne. When Gillian was a schoolgirl in England in the 1930s, her instructors wrote to her parents saying that they thought she had a learning disorder because she was constantly fidgeting and had difficulty concentrating.

Gillian's mother took her to see a specialist. For nearly 20 minutes the eight-year-old sat on her hands while her mother described all of her school difficulties to the doctor. Finally, the doctor told Gillian to wait in the room while he spoke with her mother privately in the hallway. Before the doctor left the room with Gillian's mother, he turned on the radio sitting on his desk. In the hallway he asked Gillian's mother to observe her daughter through a one-way mirror. She had risen to her feet the moment the two left the room, and had begun dancing to the music. After they watched Gillian for a short time, this remarkable doctor advised, "Mrs. Lynne, Gillian isn't sick, she's a dancer. Take her to a dance school."

Lynne's mother took the doctor's advice and enrolled her in a dance school, where Gillian discovered there were other people just like her who had to move to think. She eventually auditioned and earned a spot in the Royal Ballet School, founded her own dance company, and worked with Andrew Lloyd Webber as the choreographer of such Broadway theatre hits as *Cats* and *The Phantom of the Opera*. Robinson points out that Gillian Lynne has been responsible for some of the most memorable theater productions in history, has given pleasure to millions, and has become a multimillionaire. A different doctor, Robinson observes, may have put young Gillian on medication and told her to calm down.

Accommodating a student's readiness and abilities, therefore, is a critical starting point in successfully differentiating instruction for that student, making the learning process more joyful for everyone.

What does it mean to differentiate based on students' social needs? According to Carol Ann Tomlinson (1995), teachers can create "readiness-based adjustments" that provide students with a variety of learning tasks developed along one or more of the following continua:

Readiness-based Adjustments

1. **Concrete to abstract.** As they advance, learners benefit from tasks that involve more abstract materials, representations, ideas, or applications. For example, a teacher discussing the 13 stripes on the American flag could move from the flag to a map of the original colonies to a discussion of democracy.

2. **Simple to complex.** As they advance, learners benefit from tasks that are more complex in resources, research, issues, problems, skills, and goals. For example, a teacher could ask students to create American flags. Next, the teacher could read aloud stories about the American flag and ask students to write essays about the flag's evolution. Later, students could work in small groups using Internet tools to create a WebQuest that teaches a unit on the origins and history of the American flag.

3. **Basic to transformational.** As they advance, learners benefit from tasks that require greater transformation or manipulation of information, ideas, materials, and applications.

4. **Fewer facets to multifacets.** As they advance, learners benefit from tasks that have more facets or parts in their directions, connections within or across subjects, or planning and execution of learning activities.

5. **Smaller leaps to greater leaps.** As they advance, learners benefit from tasks that require greater mental leaps in insight, application, and transfer.

6. **More structured to more open.** As they advance, learners benefit from tasks that are more open in regard to solutions, decisions, and approaches.

7. **Less independence to greater independence.** As they advance, learners benefit from greater independence in planning, designing, and self-monitoring.

8. **Faster to slower.** As they advance, learners benefit from rapid movement through prescribed materials and tasks. At other times, they may require a greater amount of time with a given study than less advanced peers so that they may explore the topic in greater depth and/or breadth.

Thus, the question becomes, how do teachers get to know students' readiness—their strengths and weaknesses—in order to identify their social needs?

Quick Strategies to Help Teachers Identify Students' Needs

1. **Grab student files.** While knowing a student's previous educational history can sometimes impede a teacher's expectations, good teachers seek information about their students' cultural backgrounds, preferred learning styles, language proficiency levels, and more.

2. **Send home surveys.** Parents can provide critical information to teachers about students' backgrounds. Ask parents to share how students act at home, student likes/dislikes and any other relevant information that can help their student excel in your classroom.

3. **Distribute learning style inventories to students.** Ask students directly which strategies work best for them. It is often just as beneficial for students to reflect on their own learning styles as it is for teachers to determine how best to meet students' needs.

4. **Assess without stress.** Offer students a variety of assessment options, designed with various proficiency levels, learning styles, and thinking skills in mind. Assessments need to provide ongoing feedback to students in concrete ways that let them know how to improve. Assessments should vary from teacher observation and test tools (multiple choice, short essay, fill-in-the-blank), to student-generated performances, displays, etc.

5. **Understand that variety is the spice of life!** Hold a clipboard and observe students as they work alone, with partners, and in small groups. Pay attention to how students respond to different situations and make notes to better inform how you teach each student.

This chapter talks about some of the tricks you can use to identify and promote the social needs of individual students.

Fifteen Ways to Meet Your Love and Belonging Needs

 Encourage Often

We have a responsibility to encourage students. There is a difference between *praise* and *encouragement*. Praising children with general compliments (e.g., "you look nice today") is overused, while encouraging students with specific feedback is often overlooked. Author Po Bronson (2002) has identified empty praise as a negative thing. Empty praise is the general praise that often proves meaningless to children. What they want is specific feedback. It is empty praise to tell a child "good job," but it is direct encouragement to praise a child on the way he or she took the time to write neatly.

Coaches are great teachers because they constantly provide specific feedback. If a basketball player shoots the ball well, a good coach encourages him or her by complimenting the player's follow-through motion or quick release. If a player is getting out-rebounded, a coach can immediately show the player how to "box out," and encourage the player as he or she practices the move. Praise is great, but encouragement is much more meaningful.

Sportswriter Rick Reilly wrote a wonderful story about encouragement that took place at a high school football game in Grapevine, Texas (2008). When the Gainesville State School players came out to take the field, the

Grapevine Faith fans—yes, the other team's fans—made a spirit line for them to run through. The Faith fans even made banners to cheer on Gainesville. Though Gainesville lost to Faith by 19 points, the Gainesville students were so happy that after the game they gave their winless head coach a sideline squirt-bottle shower. So what gives?

It turns out that Gainesville State School is a maximum-security correctional facility about 75 miles north of Dallas. Its football team was 0–8 and had scored only two touchdowns all year. This team from juvenile hall played with battered equipment. Faith's football team had 70 players, 11 coaches, and the latest equipment, and they boasted a 7–2 record going into the game. But Faith's head coach wanted to do something kind for the Gainesville team, so he sent out an email asking for half of Faith's fans—for one night only—to cheer for the other team. "Here's the message I want you to send," the coach wrote. "You are just as valuable as any other person on planet Earth."

When a Faith player asked his coach why they were doing this, his coach responded, "Imagine if you didn't have a home life. Imagine if everybody had pretty much given up on you. Now imagine what it would mean for hundreds of people to suddenly believe in you."

For one night, hundreds of fans and cheerleaders in a Texas town showed a group of kids—written off by most everyone else—that they were just as important and special as anyone. When the Gainesville coach met Faith's coach, he grabbed him hard by the shoulders. "You'll never know what your people did for these kids tonight," he said. "You'll never, ever know."

As the Gainesville team drove back to their juvenile detention facility, players looked out the window in awe at these strangers who waved and clapped and smiled at them. Someone had smiled and cheered for them!

In a day and age where we are so readily exposed to all the horrible things humans are capable of, isn't it nice from time to time to see the impact we can have with these simple acts of kindness? Little things can make a big difference.

 ## Pray or Meditate

Prayer is hope. No matter how or to whom you pray, prayer offers reflection and meditation, two much-needed and underutilized commodities in schools today.

My mentor, Mrs. Turner, used to lead a prayer circle after school every day. Mrs. Turner was no-nonsense, and would hold hands with us and plead, "Oh Lord, please help these stupid children." She was not trying to be mean; she simply thought the only knowledge her children would ever receive would come from her classroom. Wow. Isn't that an amazing burden she shouldered every day? She knew she could not do it alone, and that is why she prayed.

I was surrounded by older African American women teachers, and yet they included me in a way that has always endeared them to me. Some people wonder if teachers in the inner cities need to carry a gun. The very idea just makes me laugh. How is a gun a remedy for anything? Instead, why don't we ask teachers to carry a Bible if they feel threatened? Plenty of shady characters mess with people toting guns, more than they would with someone toting a Bible.

What I learned from Mrs. Turner was that holding students in your thoughts was a great way to show love for others and give them a sense of belonging. Try praying for your students. You may be amazed to find that it gives you strength and makes you a kinder, gentler teacher. What many find comforting in prayer is that it offers hope, and that is one thing of which schools can never have enough.

⇨ Bowl

When I first became a teacher, some fellow teachers and I would go bowling. One friend proposed that anyone who could not bowl 100 had to buy a round of drinks for everyone. Ironically, he was the person who could never seem to break 100. To me, if you're looking for a way to have a good time, there is no better activity than bowling. It is a great way to blow off steam.

If you do not want to bowl, figure out another activity, like playing Scrabble® or taking hikes. I once had a professor who took us to baseball games, restaurants, and on nature hikes. Not only did I love him as a professor, I found myself learning more in his class because his opinion mattered to me. Since he was interested in the same subject he taught, I wanted to be interested in the subject. He earned my respect and devotion by showing my classmates and me that he could talk to us about many topics besides school. I think kids and adults both need that.

You may find some of the best learning that takes place in the classroom occurs after playing with students on the playground or hanging out with them after school, talking about sports or movies. Occasionally interrupt a stale lesson with a contest to see which student can make a "basket" in the trash can with wadded pieces of paper. It only takes a few minutes, and it is a good way to refocus students on the lesson. These experiences, like bowling together, provide us with a light, unifying experience. In the movie *Remember the Titans* (2000)—the story of a white, Southern school integrating African American students—an African American coach takes over the football team, and all the players and coaches go away to football camp for a couple of weeks. The camp begins with plenty of tension, but by the time the team returns home, the players are united. You may see the same effect after taking students on field trips. Field trips are becoming more rare, but those trips always seem to help students and teachers form a common bond with each other.

No matter the experience, it is important for people to share experiences together. This extra bonding can pay huge dividends in the ways it builds camaraderie.

 ## Become a Mentor

Here is a story I once heard about Alexander the Great:

> One day, a beggar along the roadside asked for alms as Alexander the Great was passing by in his caravan. Alexander threw the man several gold coins, much to the astonishment of those in his party. "Your Highness, copper coins would have adequately met that beggar's need," one of Alexander's servants said. "Why give him gold?" Alexander smiled and nodded. "Of course copper coins would have suited the beggar's need," Alexander replied. "But gold coins suit my giving."

The true path to joy in the classroom runs along a road of kindness. One of the most unselfish acts an experienced teacher can bestow is to mentor a beginning teacher. Beginning teachers may be in their first year or in their fourth year. When you see a colleague who needs some assistance, offer help. Most successful people learned the ropes at the side of a mentor. Teaching is like any other profession or skill: it takes time to master. It is not boastful to offer expertise to someone in need. Most teachers who mentor beginning, struggling, or student teachers stand to gain nothing, and that is true generosity. They share their knowledge, and sometimes they even learn a thing or two from "newbies." The generosity of mentoring says more about the giver than about the one who receives. So be generous with your time and resources, and pass along your talents to others.

Team Teach

Working with a colleague is a great way to connect. My mentor, friend, and neighbor, Mrs. Turner, used to team teach with me, and we both learned so much from one another. One of my more challenging boys, Francisco, had a knack for getting on different teachers' nerves and grinding away. One of his favorite games to play was "I'm not so smart." I figured out his strategy pretty quickly, and I managed to reverse the game, to "Let me prove to you how smart I am." I was so happy that I had figured out a way to get through to him. It took several months, but there was a way to reach him.

Mrs. Turner did not exactly share my patience with Francisco. One day, I saw Mrs. Turner standing over Francisco. She began pointing to his paper, as if she were counting something. Then, I heard Mrs. Turner let out a huge sigh of exasperation. "Child, you have 13 letters in your first and last names," she said. "If you get your name, you'll know half the alphabet." That is still one of the funniest things I have ever heard a teacher say to a child. It may not be the most politically correct anecdote, but most teachers can empathize because they have had a similar student or situation.

Why don't more teachers team teach, or at least observe each other? Observing teachers and practicing lessons together is essential to good teaching. Too many teachers lesson-plan in solitude. Why? Work with someone who can introduce a new twist, or show you an old trick. If you are the veteran, share the wealth! Let teachers in on your secrets, and point them towards the resources that you found to be most helpful. In Norris School District in Bakersfield, California, elementary schools are designed with grade-level "pods" allowing teachers to observe their colleagues without interrupting their classes. Collaboration is present everywhere, and the district claims this is one of the reasons for its high rate of teacher retention.

Author Peter Drucker (2007) tells a terrific story about the chemist Robert Boyle. Boyle created an engine that used the explosion of gunpowder to drive the piston, but this fouled the cylinder so much it had to be taken apart and cleaned after each stoke. Boyle's idea, however, enabled his assistant, Denis Papin, to continue to refine the idea, which inspired inventor Thomas Newcomen. In 1712, Newcomen built the first steam engine that actually performed useful work. It pumped the water out of an English coal mine. However, James Watt is considered the inventor of the steam engine. Why? Watt's steam engine was simply more refined. Boyle had the idea, and the others built on that foundation. That is the same principle of good teaching. Good teachers help one another out, and great teachers give praise to one another. It takes a team effort.

When pitcher Lefty Gomez was inducted into the Baseball Hall of Fame, a reporter asked him, "Lefty, what was your secret?" Lefty smiled. "Two things;" he said, "clean living and a fast infield." Nobody is successful alone. Every successful person builds on a foundation others have laid.

 Write It Down

How do you feel when your principal says you're doing a good job? Pretty good, huh? Now, how do you feel when your principal writes you a note acknowledging all of your efforts? You probably keep that note in a file forever. Most teachers need encouragement almost as much as they need a raise. Make it a point to tell your colleagues (including your administrators) how much you appreciate them, and write it down. They need that support as much as your students do.

People respond well to verbal praise and encouragement, but writing those thoughts down can leave a lasting impact. Students, in particular, crave the raves of adults.

Leave sticky notes all over the place for your students. One student may open his desk and find a sticky note complimenting him on how neat he is keeping his desk. Another student might find a sticky note in her cubbyhole thanking her for being such an outstanding and supportive group leader. You can even leave sticky notes inside students' books telling them how proud you are that they are reading so much. The grins you see will surely compensate you for time and money spent on sticky notes. Sticky notes produce happy students.

Here's an idea: At your first meeting with parents, hand each parent a sticky note pad and show them a bulletin board of praise and encouragement in your classroom. Every week, ask parents to fill out a sticky note for their child to encourage him or her on an upcoming assignment, and also write a sticky note to praise their child for an accomplishment over the previous week. Most parents are great and take the time to write a couple of sticky notes, like "Pablo, Mama and I are so proud of you. Keep on improving on those spelling tests," or "Sayed, you can be anything you want if you try your best, and never give up. Love, Mommy." If you have reluctant parents, write some yourself and tell students that a mystery parent likes to write sticky notes. That way you can encourage all students. You will find the sticky notes are a great way to share your love for your students and acknowledge all of their efforts.

Everyone needs a pat on the back. Take it a step further, and write it down.

 ## Keep Up with Social Networking

You are not alone. Too many teachers leave the profession in their first three years, probably because they do not receive the proper support. A teacher who struggles usually does not realize that there is something happening beyond his or her control. In the Internet age, it is essential for teachers to support one another, to share the tribulations and triumphs of teachers of all ages, even if it is in communities such as blogs, online forums or Facebook, which offer abundant tips.

When people outside of education ask how teachers are doing, I usually tell them that out of every 100 teachers I observe, perhaps 10 should go back to their old jobs; two belong in federal institutions (by the way, these are the two that the media likes to devote most of its attention to); 15 need to be issued superhero capes—I would do anything to get my own children in their classrooms; and the remaining 73 teachers are pretty good. They may not be good at everything, but they are workable. With some time and coaching, a lot of average teachers can grow into stellar teachers.

We lose too many good teachers because they give 110 percent and very few people take the time to acknowledge their efforts. It is usually not the teacher's fault that he or she burns out. Perhaps the person is teaching the wrong grade level. Many mediocre eighth grade teachers excel as elementary school teachers, and vice versa. Maybe they are at the wrong school. Plenty of teachers who burned out in the inner city flourish in the suburbs, and vice versa. Some teachers are pushed into assignments that are not the right fit. Every now and then teachers do get a class of students with whom they do not connect very well. Many teachers do not know that they are not alone.

Social networks provide teachers with an additional outlet to air their grievances or inquire about ways to reach certain students. Teaching, in many ways, can be quite isolating, and a lot of teachers become introverts who undervalue their own expertise. Do yourself a favor and offer your expertise to others. Share your knowledge online. You might be surprised how the act of offering your own trials and tribulations to others through teacher chat rooms, blogs, wikis, etc., often yields as many significant benefits to you as to others.

Join Potlucks

A wonderful folktale to share with students is *Stone Soup*, a story about some hungry soldiers who visit a town where no one is willing to feed them. The soldiers start making their favorite stone soup and, at the soldiers' suggestions, curious villagers offer various ways to add flavors that would make this particular batch perfect. Before long, the entire village has contributed something to the pot, and now they all have a feast.

The term potluck reportedly comes from the practice of never throwing anything away. In medieval times, it was a common practice at taverns and inns to preserve meal leftovers in a pot. It was kept warm in order to feed unforeseen guests. When a person arrived for a meal, they were given "the luck of the pot." In the same way, any good teacher realizes that what does not work today should be filed away for another day because it may work beautifully with another group of students in the future.

Food is a wonderful way to bring people together. You will attract parents to weekly parent workshops after school by offering free food. When people hear the words *free* and *food* placed together, they tend to bring their extended families. It may cost a little bit of money in the beginning, but after a while, weekly workshops tend to turn into potlucks and fiestas that bring the families of students together. The little bit of money you invest at first can pay huge dividends, as you may find parents to be much more supportive of your efforts once they understand you are all on the same team.

Potlucks are also a great way to bring a school's faculty and staff together. I taught with many African American women, and we used to have a soul food potluck once a semester. There were plenty of meetings where people moaned and left early, but the soul food potlucks always lasted for hours and boasted nothing but laughter and sharing. So administrators, take heed: The next time you need to boost enthusiasm at a faculty meeting, host a potluck.

 Give Daily Compliments

Art Linkletter used to host a great show based on his best-selling book called *Kids Say the Darndest Things* (2005). The show was filled with positive, clean, innocent humor— something in rare supply nowadays. Once, Linkletter interviewed a girl in first grade. "What does love look like?" he asked her. The little girl thought and answered, "It's when I let Johnny get in front of me at the drinking fountain line." Linkletter smiled. "Well, you must love Johnny very much," he said. The little girl shook her head, and said, "No, I don't even like him."

That little girl epitomizes love. A great book says that "love is patient," and "love is kind." If you want your students to all feel like they belong, encourage random acts of kindness. One great teaching strategy came from a second grade teacher in Japan. She would end every day by asking students to stand and talk about another student who helped them throughout the day. Another teacher gives her kindergartners five pennies to place in their right-hand pockets. Every time students compliment a classmate, they place a penny in their left-hand pocket. At the end of the day the teacher asks students how many pennies they have in their left-hand pockets. How often do you direct students' attention to kindness?

Go out of your way every day to thank somebody. Go out of your way to compliment somebody. You will reap the benefits of your positive energy.

Read and Write Poetry

In Homer's epic poem, *The Odyssey* (n.d.), the sirens were mythical, evil creatures—half-bird and half-woman—who lived on an island surrounded by submerged, jagged rocks. As ships approached the island, the sirens would sing beautiful, seductive songs, luring the sailors to their deaths. When Odysseus' ship approached the island, he ordered his crew to fill their ears with wax to escape the lure of the sirens' songs. Then he commanded them to bind him to the mast as they passed the island so he could not change his orders. On another occasion, however, when Orpheus sailed his ship by that same island, he sang a song of his own that was so beautiful and divine that his sailors did not even listen to the sirens' music.

What kind of music do you create for your classroom? Do you try to help them ignore the negative noise around them, or do you overpower the negativity with some positive music of your own?

Read poems with your students, and do so enthusiastically. If it takes barely five minutes of class time throughout the school day, then over the course of 180 school days, students will have heard over 700 poems. They will begin to love to read and write poetry and songs. Share your passions with your students, and you will be surprised how they will begin to share those same passions with you. Try starting with this excerpt from a poem by Emily Dickinson:

"I'm Nobody! Who Are You?"
By Emily Dickinson (1978)

I'm nobody! Who are you?

Are you nobody, too?

Then there's a pair of us—don't tell!

They'd banish us, you know.

How dreary to be somebody!

How public, like a frog

To tell your name the livelong day

To an admiring bog!

Reading Dickinson, one gets the feeling she had a pretty low opinion of herself. Did you know that Emily Dickinson never shared her poetry while she was alive? It's true: they found all of her poems in her attic after her death. This woman had no idea how much joy she would give the world with her poetry. Tell your students that all of them were put on Earth to share their poetry.

While you may be hard-pressed to find sufficient evidence about the need for belonging, this is a common theme in novels, autobiographies, plays, and especially poetry. By encouraging students to write about their experiences and share them with their classmates, you can gain valuable insights into what your students feel. This helps you serve your students better.

 Tend Your Flock

A football coach once told his players that they had a choice to be one of two things: a bag of marbles or a bag of grapes. When a confused player asked him what he meant, the coach elaborated. "A bag of marbles consists of individual units that do not affect one another unless colliding," he said. "At any moment, any member of this team can choose to skip a practice or weight-training session, since no one really cares whether there are 55 or 56 marbles in a bag." Then the coach looked at his players and asked them if they wanted to be a bag of grapes. "The juices begin to mingle, and there is no way to extricate yourselves if you tried," the coach said. "Each is part of all, and each individually contributes to the overall fragrance."

One of the reasons NBA basketball coach Phil Jackson was so successful is because he ensures that his twelfth man on the bench feels just as important as Kobe Bryant or Michael Jordan to the success of his team. Your students need to believe that they are part of your herd, your flock, your posse—whatever you want to call yourselves.

Too many people underplay the deep importance of belonging. Make your kids feel like they are supposed to be there, and encourage them to learn the importance of supporting one another. This is just as important, if not more important, in middle and high school as it is in elementary school.

There's a story about a high school basketball player who lost his mother to cancer earlier in the day but decided to play in his team's game that night. He showed up in the second quarter and—since his coach had left him off the roster, thinking he would not play—his team was assessed a mandatory technical foul. When the opposing team took the two free throws, they intentionally missed both, out of empathy for the opposing player's tragic loss. There are plenty of coaches who produce professional-caliber basketball players; I pray that my own children have a coach who produces such professional-caliber human beings.

 ## Enlist Big Buddies

Competence produces confidence. Confidence produces joy. Do you remember the television show *Little House on the Prairie* (1974)? Did you ever notice the school

Laura attended was a single room, and the students in that classroom were all sizes and ages?

Who had the bright idea to classify students by age? That is about as random as classifying students by shoe size. Just because kids are the same age means very little, as students grow at their own rates. Any elementary school teacher will attest that the cognitive development of boys is very different than that of girls.

One way to get kids excited about school is through peer tutoring. Take a low fifth grade reader and match that student with a low first grader. Both will be better readers after they work together, and both will like school a whole lot more. Students who are your biggest discipline problems can turn into stellar scholars as a result of peer tutoring. Everybody needs to feel important.

If it is too difficult to facilitate peer tutoring in your school, recognize the diverse abilities of students within any classroom. Just because Precious is an excellent reader does not necessarily mean she is a stellar mathematician, and Miguel—a lower-level reader—may be able to assist Precious with her math while she helps his reading. Again, good teachers publicly acknowledge the strengths of every individual student to show the class that everybody has a talent that contributes to the overall success of the class.

 Communicate Face-to-Face

A mother text messages her son that she received a voicemail from her secretary regarding a recent email from his teacher, and he "tweets" her later about a comment that he posted on Facebook criticizing his teacher's blog.

Have you ever called someone and been startled when they picked up the phone and answered? And have you ever asked that person to hang up so you could call back and leave a voicemail? Some people admit that the reason they send text messages is to avoid getting "stuck" on the phone in a conversation. Has society become that impersonal?

Technology is great in so many ways, yet society has lost a lot of intimacy because of technology. Voicemail, email, and text messages have replaced conversations and other forms of face-to-face communication between teachers, students, parents, and administrators. Overwhelmed by standardized testing and mountains of paperwork, too many teachers have lost the time to get to know their students' feelings and aspirations.

Children, in particular, yearn for contact, for belonging to a group. Group membership enables children to overcome feelings of alienation, awkwardness, and isolation caused by a multitude of issues. Incorporating more time for students to talk with teachers and one another is a way to build better classrooms.

Society has changed. Kids do not play outside after school anymore. Their parents arrange "play dates." Families no longer eat dinner together, as their staggered schedules find dad working late, mom going to her pilates class, brother attending baseball practice, and sister rehearsing her school play. Meanwhile, in Europe, people will often hang out at an outdoor café for hours, talking with one another and "people-watching." Researchers at UCLA found that human beings require no less than eight physical contacts (hugs, handshakes, pats on the back, etc.) every day. Computers, television, and video games are capable of many things, but they cannot hug a child. Facilitating plenty of opportunities for students to interact is a great way to build unity in a classroom. You will find greater satisfaction as a teacher by building deeper relationships with your students, their parents, and your colleagues.

Listen

Be honest with yourself. When a person talks to you, are you listening to that person or waiting for your turn to speak? So many problems in society could be resolved if people learned to become active listeners. A lot of people are not so much looking for an answer to their problems as much as an empathetic shoulder to cry on.

There are five levels of listening:

Level 1—I am not listening.

Level 2—I interrupt or disagree.

Level 3—I tell you what I think.

Level 4—This is what I hear you saying. Tell me more.

Level 5—This is what I think you are saying. I wonder how you might be feeling?

These levels provide a pretty good rubric to rate how well one listens. Here are some listening techniques to help teachers, students, and anyone else become better listeners:

1. **Stop talking.** You cannot listen to someone while you are talking.

2. **Empathize.** Put yourself in the other person's shoes and see the situation from his or her point of view.

3. **Ask open-ended questions.** Find out the person's needs.

4. **Do not interrupt.** Let him or her freely express him or herself.

5. **Concentrate.** Actively focus your attention on words, ideas, and feelings. Look the person in the eye.

6. **React to ideas, not the person.** Do not let personal opinion influence your interpretation of

what is said.

7. **Avoid mental arguing.** You cannot listen while engaged in a mental debate.

8. **Listen for personality.** Find out what his/her likes, dislikes, value systems, and motivations are.

9. **Avoid hasty judgments.** It is important to have all the facts and to be open-minded.

10. **Try not to fake your attention.** The speaker's self-esteem is at stake here. Often that is exactly what someone needs—your attention.

You can do a much better job serving students, their parents, and colleagues by following these guidelines when listening.

 Open Your Door

It does not take long to understand how a school operates. Any seasoned educator can get a sense of a school within five minutes simply by observing classroom doors. Are they open? Is the principal's door open? Are doors colorful or dreary? Doors tell us a lot about the environments we want to promote. Do you want to create a warm, welcoming community or stand as an isolated island?

Keep your door open. Offer colleagues supplies. Despite the loss of supplies to you, it could turn out to be a real blessing to show some kindness to your colleagues in this way. People who never help anyone else may suddenly be willing to help you, all because you took the first step by showing a bit of collegiality. Consider it something you want to model to your students: If you want the world to be better, you have to be better. Gandhi put it best when he said, "Be the change you seek."

Teachers are notorious hoarders. They are a lot like the character Milton in the film *Office Space* (1999) who snags a stapler and cherishes it like Gollum's ring in Tolkien's *The Lord of the Rings*. Have you ever come across teachers who have stockpiles of crayons hidden in their classrooms as if they were awaiting a nuclear holocaust where they would have crayons and no one else would? That is no way to live. You have to relax and offer whatever you can to your neighbors. Open your door and offer whatever you have, and you might be surprised how much goodwill follows.

Reflection Questions

1. Generosity is the mark of a joyful teacher. So, do you give your colleagues copper coins, or do you shower them with gold?

2. A pretty song that kindergartners sing says, "Each of us is a flower, growing high in our garden." What can we do to make sure we nurture our students and provide them with roots to assure them that they belong?

3. What are three things you are doing to make your students feel like they belong? What are three more things you could be doing?

Esteem Needs

Overview

Read the two scenarios and think about the self-esteem of the students in each case.

Scenario 1:

A third grade teacher asks a boy about his favorite sport. The boy's eyes light up, his entire body seems to straighten up, and he enthusiastically exclaims, "I like soccer!" "Really," the teacher replies. "That's a nice sport, but I think basketball is better. Why don't we read about basketball?" The boy nods slightly as his teacher smiles and shows him a book about NBA basketball stars. As the teacher works with the boy, the boy's body slides deeper and deeper beneath his desk, while his bright smile fades into a series of polite nods.

Scenario 2:

When a fourth grade teacher informs her students that they will be examining the cultures of Native Americans, scattered moans and groans fill the class. The teacher provides a list of standards and objectives which they will need to cover and asks students to partner with a classmate and brainstorm ideas for activities to make the topic more interesting. She leads a whole-class brainstorm at the whiteboard and writes every idea students suggest under the objective or standard that matches the idea. Afterwards, she asks students if there is at least one activity which they find interesting, under each objective. Once the class agrees, she asks students to select an activity that they would like to perform for each objective and encourages students to work in small groups. The teacher adds that she is interested to see which group can put together the most interesting project. Students move desks to get together, and the room's noise level increases several decibels as students consult one another about how to create the most interesting project.

Which classroom would you rather be in? In the first one, the teacher asks for the student's interest but guides the student to an activity that reflects the teacher's interest. In the second, the teacher listens to students' concerns and challenges them to find ways to make interesting projects from a topic they perceived to be dull. She does not tell students what an interesting project should look like, yet her students promptly form small groups to discuss possibilities. While student input is solicited but ignored in one class, it is sought, greeted, and encouraged in another.

Everyone needs to be respected. Everyone wants to engage in activities that give them a sense of contribution and purpose. That feeling of worth contributes significantly to a child's self-esteem. No teacher can serve students effectively without determining and building upon the interests of those students. Teachers who manage successful differentiated classrooms continuously monitor their students' interests, and with interest comes joy. When a teacher successfully identifies topics that evoke passion in students, he or she is more likely to engage the students in learning. If the bell rings but the students stay in their seats because they want to finish whatever it is they are doing, that teacher has found something that excites the students.

To effectively differentiate a classroom's environment, content to be covered, activities, and final learning products, you need to build on the interests of your students. The challenge for teachers, therefore, is to start over every year. Every student is different. Every class is different. A class that respects those differences is a class that fosters high self-esteem for students by letting them feel valued and successful.

So what does it mean to differentiate based on student interests?

Quick Strategies to Help Teachers Meet Students' Esteem Needs

1. **Provide choices.** Providing students with choice is essential to building their self-esteem in the differentiated classroom. Good teachers can observe students' choices and better understand students' interests and then design activities that best suit these students.

2. **Survey students.** Teachers can find out directly from students about their interests through questioning, thumbs up/thumbs down, interest surveys, etc. To mix things up a bit, try incorporating movement into surveys (e.g., ask students to go to different corners of the room based on whether they agree, disagree, strongly agree, or strongly disagree with a statement; provide students with "yes or no" or "true or false" statements and ask them to walk to the appropriate half of the classroom).

3. **Hug it out!** Students who are encouraged tend to show more interest. Good teachers are generous at encouraging students and celebrating students' growth with hugs, high fives, pats on the back, etc. Remember, humans need physical affirmation as much as verbal.

4. **Build competency.** When students feel like they are good at something, they tend to become more motivated to continue working hard. Put students in positive settings that build on their strengths. Positive settings are safe settings—they encourage students to take risks. Point out each student's proficiency to the entire class, and ask students to lead mini-lessons, activities, etc.

5. **Keep the brain in mind.** Brain research shows that the brain is stimulated through water, oxygen, music, and movement. Keep students' interest level high by getting them moving around as much as possible. Water and restroom breaks should be frequently used as transition activities. I think music and laughter are characteristics of highly engaged classrooms.

6. **Pass the buck.** Students' interest and esteem are greatly enhanced when they feel in control of situations. As often as possible, let students be in charge. Students can lead morning meetings, facilitate discussions, and perform classroom routines (e.g., taking attendance or checking homework).

7. **Make it relevant.** One way to build students' interest in a topic is to demonstrate how useful that skill will be in their day-to-day lives. Obscure concepts waste everyone's time. The teacher who can ensure three ideas stick in students' memories every day is doing a good job, if they can get those concepts to stick. One of the ways to do that is to relate concepts to students' lives (e.g., adding can be supplemented with how teams score in various sports; a lesson on democracy is more meaningful if the teacher allows students to vote on classroom decisions).

8. **Increase feedback.** Have you ever had a coach tell you that he was so hard on you because he thought highly of you and believed you had the potential to get better? Good teachers provide ongoing feedback to let students know whether they are on the right or wrong path. Indifference is a sure way to destroy students' self-esteem. It is also a good idea to keep a clipboard so you can immediately note feedback and keep track of how much feedback you provide individual students.

9. **Invoke the Santa Clause.** Ask students in pairs to give one another their "wish lists" for the types of activities or subjects that they would like in their ideal classroom. Teachers who try to build classrooms around their students' interests tend to be much more successful.

10. **Engage in teacher talk.** Teachers should ask their students about their favorite television shows, video games, etc., and build their classroom environments, content, processes, and products accordingly. Again, building on students' interests is one of the best ways to boost their self-esteem and confidence.

This chapter shows some ways to meet the esteem needs of individual students.

Fifteen Ways to Meet Your Self-Esteem Needs

 ### Incorporate Game Playing

Supposedly, the average American can sit and listen for about 17 minutes—give or take 17 minutes. That means teachers have to keep things moving. Everyone should teach kindergartners at some point. Kindergartners require constant stimulation. Their minds jump around more frequently than fleas on a poodle. Any good kindergarten teacher knows that the day should include plenty of high-interest games. Kindergarten, in fact, is the "New York, New York" of public education: If you can make it there, you can make it anywhere. Additionally, the teachers who incorporate more games in their classrooms tend to be much happier and last much longer than those who robotically drill students on standards for tests.

Games need to build on students' interests. Very few students are great at everything, but every student is good at something. Teachers need to incorporate games that keep students interested in class. Like it or not, teachers are salespeople who are selling learning every day. There's no business like show business, and our job is to keep students from turning the channel.

Incorporating games throughout the day does not have to take a lot of time, either. Preferably, activities should take three to five minutes. While many would argue that it is a waste of valuable instructional time, consider this: If you teach one standard over the course of an hour, and students' attention drifts off a third of the way into your lesson, what is the likelihood that your students retain any of that information? On the other hand, why not try teaching the standard in three segments (each segment reinforcing the other), broken up by games that stimulate the mind? Games may seem trivial, but when used as a way to relax the brain they can prove to be as effective as a short breather for an athlete.

So, how do you do it? It takes time to find lots of engaging activities, and the best teachers build their repertoires over a period of years. Beginning teachers should not fret. Try out a couple of games to begin with, and note how much more students retain and how much more focused they are after playing games. Also note your own energy level. We are losing too many great teachers because of endless mandates being forced down their throats, and it is important to make school more joyful again to retain our best teachers.

 Provide Choices

Suppose a typical elementary school teacher is teaching approximately seven lessons each day. And suppose that teacher is trying to find six to eight ways to differentiate each of those lessons. That is approximately 50 types of differentiation a day. Multiply that over the course of a 180-day school year, and that is about 9,000 forms of differentiated instruction each year.

Sound daunting? It can be. Again, beginning teachers need to keep in mind that it takes time to perfect techniques and become an outstanding teacher. Yes, there are some people who are born teachers. They come out of the womb, and a wise man holds them in the sky in full view of society and declares in a deep voice, "Yes, you shall teach." However, most great teachers develop over time. One exceptional teacher is Rafe Esquith, a teacher at Hobart Elementary in South Los Angeles. He is the author of *Teach Like Your Hair's on Fire* (2007) and *There Are No Shortcuts* (2003), and he was featured in the PBS documentary *The Hobart Shakespeareans* (2005). He readily confesses that he was not a great teacher during his first 10 years. But his class today is one of the most inspirational classrooms you have ever seen. He constantly strives to be better, and he has honed his craft through years of trial and error.

Teachers need to be as patient with themselves as they are with their students. Superior classrooms evolve. Nothing excites me more than leading a full workshop and then spotting a 30-year veteran in the audience. When asked why he or she is there, the veteran always says, "Because I want to get better." Wow! Give me a faculty of teachers who are never complacent, always looking for ways to improve their instruction, and I will show you a school where all students excel.

Great administrators also recognize that great teachers come in all shapes and sizes. While some teachers may utilize techniques that seem unorthodox, great administrators recognize that as long as teachers produce positive results, they should get some say in how they deliver the instruction. The silliest part of the "standardization" movement in America is that it fails to recognize America's greatest strength—its diversity. North Carolina is great the way it is. It does not need to look like North Dakota. It is our differences that make this country the greatest country on the planet. Schools that provide choices for both students and teachers tend to provide more positive, happier, and more productive environments.

Connect Everything

Speaker Alan November tells a story of a fourth grade class in Boston that was learning about the American Revolution. Their teacher did not ask them to read their textbooks and summarize what they read, nor did he deliver a dry lecture. This teacher used Skype™ to teleconference with another fourth grade class in Great Britain, and over the course of the next couple of weeks students on both sides of the Atlantic heard the history of the American Revolution from the American and British points of view. In this way, students were able to understand that all events can be told in different ways, depending on one's perspective. Not only were the fourth graders excited about this topic, they spent a lot of their own time at home further researching the origins of the Revolution in order to present stronger arguments for their points of view.

Learning takes place when teachers facilitate meaningful experiences that connect to students' everyday lives. Think of the elementary schools in Singapore practicing "Singapore Math" (see http://www.singaporemath.com). Some schools work on fractions for nearly a month. A month! There are schools in America that spend less than three days on some of the same concepts. When asked about the reason for the lengthy lessons, one Singapore school's director smiled and said that his school wants students to have time to explore concepts and relate them to everyday experiences. Students at this school used fractions as they related to money, food, and sports. This school believes learning has to connect to students' interests and to real life. As a result, Singapore students consistently post some of the highest mathematics scores in the world.

Teachers are asked to teach numerous standards each year. A lot of those standards seem unrelated to students' lives. Few teachers can teach students to be interested in something that feels completely pointless. The fix is to connect everything. Science does not always have to occur in the afternoon, and language arts does not have to cease after the morning. Spend the entire day connecting concepts with one another in meaningful ways. Your classroom will be more interesting, challenging, and engaging to students, and you will have greater satisfaction than those teachers who isolate lessons because "every other teacher is teaching page 63 right now."

 ## Make It Stick

Chip and Dan Heath wrote *Made to Stick* (2007), a book that challenges readers to think about ways people learn and what keeps them engaged. Effective teaching means content stays with a person for a long time, and good teachers constantly seek ways to make teaching more engaging to students.

Admit it: There are times when your students get bored with you. Your job is to keep them interested, at all costs. Leave your pride at the door and, if need be, act like an imbecile to keep your students engaged. When my students are bored with me, I tell them I am going to ask "Australian Pete" to come teach them. I briefly leave the classroom and reenter with a cowboy strut and imaginary tip of the hat, greeting my students, "G'day, mates! I just got done puttin' another shrimp on the barbie when your teacher said you wanted me to read to you." The students go wild.

On other occasions, I tell students that a grumpy old man is coming to the classroom. I briefly leave the classroom and reenter with my hands shaking, a crooked back, and a scowl on my face, and I tell the students, "Shut up! You little bookworms!" The students go bonkers.

My first grade teacher once read us a story called *Millions of Cats* by Wanda Gag (1928). She came to a portion of the text that read:

> Hundreds of cats,
>
> Thousands of cats,
>
> Millions and billions and trillions of cats!

When she read aloud these lines with a sinister snarl and wicked scream, she scared us all. Although she risked traumatizing her kids, that lesson sure was memorable. Please do not scare the heck out of your students, but do try to make your lessons stick by infusing them with rich emotion. Look at that text, and ask students to echo you as you read it. Then ask them to recite it based on volume (read the first line in a whisper, the second in a normal voice, and the final line as a shout). You could ask students to rap it, or recite it like aliens—the possibilities are endless. Look at what you are doing: You are taking a dry concept and making it highly engaging.

Would you like to know what you taught today? Ask students' parents. Students always tell their parents what they enjoyed in class. When you can get things to stick in students' heads, you can greatly affect their attitudes and aptitudes. You should even find yourself having a lot more "fun" in your classroom, and that is just as important in your journey to becoming a great, long-lasting teacher.

 ## Use Multimedia and Technology

It is amazing that so many teachers continue to write lesson plans from scratch. Your lesson plan has already been written 500 times. It would seem to be a better use of your time to download a lesson plan off the Internet (or use a respected professional resource) and adapt it to meet the needs of your students this year, incorporating as many types of differentiation as you deem necessary.

If you really fear your computer, ask a five-year-old to help. Most students know more about the tools their computers feature than teachers. By eliciting student assistance, teachers can also grasp more of their students' interests, as well.

You can attend full-day workshops on free Internet tools for teachers, students, administrators, and parents. Since websites are constantly changing, however, it is not useful to list favorites here. The best thing a teacher can do is to set aside a time every day or week to perform random Google™ searches for materials. You would be surprised how many wonderful resources you will find. One other tip: pay attention to teen sites. You can find scores of activities by visiting sites that are designed for teenagers. These sites are often filled with brain games, personality quizzes, funny photos, and numerous other activities you can adapt and apply to your lessons to stimulate students' interest throughout the day.

Capture Students' Curiosity

One of the nation's favorite teachers of all time was a man by the name of Fred Rogers, "Mr. Rogers" (of *Mr. Rogers' Neighborhood*, 1968–2000). Mr. Rogers would stare at his watch for a few moments and sweetly state to the camera, "This is a watch." He'd pause and continue investigating his watch before kindly asking the viewing audience, "Ever wonder how watches are made?" Children all over the country would be shaking their heads and saying to the television, "No, but I want to know now!"

All Mr. Rogers had to do was take a simple piece of realia (in this case, a watch) and devote all of his attention to it, and that simple act could spark children's curiosity. Arnold Schwarzenegger utilized the same technique in the film *Kindergarten Cop* (1990). On his first day of teaching kindergartners, he had no control over his rowdy bunch of five- and six-year-old kids, until he brought in his pet ferret. Upon seeing the ferret, the students ceased their mayhem and gathered around to ask questions about the strange animal. Good teachers constantly attract the attention of their students.

Watch inspirational teaching movies. Have you ever seen one where the teacher goes into a "difficult" classroom and inspires his or her students by utilizing the mandatory scripted curricula? The best teachers capture their students' curiosities by inspiring them with poems, practicing chants, singing songs, and acting crazy. Whatever it takes, that is what great teachers do to attract students' attention. Real learning can only begin when students are interested.

 Pose Problems

Try to solve this riddle:

> What is smaller than an atom…
> Larger than infinity…
> Greater than God…
> And, if you eat it, you'll die?

The answer is "nothing," since nothing is smaller than an atom, nothing is larger than infinity, nothing is greater than God, and—if you eat nothing—you will die. While most adults take a long time and fail to come up with the answer, young children seem to have no problem at all solving the riddle. Why? Adults tend to over complicate things, which explains why so many schools implement scripted reading programs when they could have better results by simply providing students with rich, engaging literature and read-alouds.

Throughout the day, build on students' critical thinking and problem-solving skills by challenging them with riddles and puzzles. It is conceivable that most of the world's problems could be solved by a roomful of first graders if adults would just listen to their lines of reasoning. Openly encourage students to "think aloud" by talking about their thought processes and the strategies they use to solve problems. This allows other students to relate to and affirm their own thought processes and strategies. It also shows students that there can be multiple routes to an answer—or completely different and better answers.

A first grader once asked me one of the most insightful questions I had ever heard. He asked if Curious George is a monkey or an ape. Reread *Curious George* (1973). The author refers to Curious George as a monkey. But where is his tail? Most monkeys have tails, but apes do not. Be honest: In your entire life, did you ever stop to question that? Encourage students to ask lots of questions. Problem-solving activities are a great way to highlight these skills.

➡ Recognize Growth

Everybody likes to receive positive peer attention. Teachers can build student self-esteem by telling them that they are really talented at a given activity and remark specifically about how they continue to improve. The more students feel encouraged, the better they feel about trying, and the more invested they tend to become.

Peter Reynolds wrote a terrific book, *The Dot* (2003). This simple story tells of a little girl named Vashti who does not consider herself to be an artist. Her teacher encourages her to make a mark and see where it takes her. Vashti jabs her felt-tipped pen on the paper to make a dot and signs her name. The next day she is amazed to see her "dot" picture framed and hanging in the classroom. Encouraged, she starts to make more dots and exhibits all of her work to an impressed student body. When Vashti meets a boy who does not think he can draw, she encourages him to make a mark and sign his name.

Singer Jack Johnson tells a childhood story about drawing a pastel picture of a farmer in a hat with his arms crossed. His dad looked at it and said, "The toes are in the wrong place." Indeed, the toes were backward, and Johnson was crushed at first, really disappointed. Then his father added, "It makes the picture more interesting. That's your artistic license. You can choose where the big toes go!" From that moment on, Johnson says he felt empowered artistically.

What are you doing to encourage your students? Sometimes all it takes is one remark by a teacher to spark a student's passion for life. Recognizing student growth through public displays of encouragement, even something as simple as highlighting student work on a bulletin board, is a great way to promote student interest. Remember the policy of successful leaders: Praise publicly and reprimand privately. Celebrate how much students grow. Have you ever measured a child's growth in height on a wall? Why not show students how much they have learned over the course of a year, month or week? Learning is empowering, and too often students (and teachers, for that matter) fail to acknowledge how far they have come.

Seek Input

Students are much more excited about learning when they feel they have a hand in it. Give students ownership and build on their interests by asking them to choose what will be learned today, how it will be learned, and how to demonstrate that they have learned it. There is a teacher who writes each standard to be taught on a strip of paper. One group of students selects the standard(s) of the day and places the standard(s) on the sentence-strip holder. Another group follows the same procedure for activities, while another group selects the different products that will be produced. All of this takes place at the morning meeting. Classroom visitors can readily sense the excitement the class feels when they play such an important role in their daily agenda.

Good teachers are not threatened by handing over control of the class to their students. They have trained their students how to be responsible for their own learning. Train students on procedures, and then let them have a say about how to improve systems. The more students are empowered to run the class, the better.

Be humble. You do not know everything. Get over it. Encourage input, and seek ways to make your classroom better. Talk to colleagues and administrators. Consult parents. Even the school secretary and janitor can offer a wealth of information. The school was not built for you; it was built for students. Teachers are there for students, period. You need to hand them as much responsibility as you can in order to make them feel accountable to themselves, one another, and you. Think of it as building pride of ownership.

Share Stories

Rick Wormeli is one of education's most gifted presenters, offering practical and classroom-tested strategies in a fun and engaging way. When speaking to audiences he has the ability to drive home points by sharing anecdotes from his classrooms and those of others. His stories leave lasting impressions that slide show bullet points fail to offer. You can disseminate as much information as you want, but if you do not present the information in a compelling and meaningful way, the message is lost.

Ken Blanchard and Spencer Johnson understood this better than anybody when they wrote *The One-Minute Manager* (1982), a parable written to demonstrate good business practices in a meaningful way to business people. Since publication of that best-seller, the market has been flooded with simple stories for business people to remember, rather than the old-fashioned, conventional books of best practices in business, which tend to present elaborate lists of characteristics readers never seem to remember. In taking a page from their book, I have read aloud countless children's picture books to business executives to demonstrate ways to improve communication and team-building in their businesses.

To maintain students' interest, share stories with them. Try reading aloud short stories from Paul Harvey's *The Rest of the Story* mystery/history books (1976). Share your own personal stories to engage your students. Keep things simple, and it is amazing how much more people retain.

 Show How You Know

Remember the movie *Butch Cassidy and the Sundance Kid* (1969)? There is a scene in the movie where Butch (Paul Newman) and Sundance (Robert Redford) are trying to get legitimate jobs in Bolivia. They approach a man who needs someone to protect him when he brings back a payroll by mule. The proprietor tosses a can and asks Sundance to shoot it, and Sundance draws his gun rapidly and starts to move. The man puts his hand on Sundance and says, "No, don't move, son. Just shoot the can." Sundance aims, fires, and misses. Butch cannot believe it, because he has never seen Sundance miss in his life. "Can I move?" Sundance asks the man, and before he answers, Sundance rapidly draws his gun and hits the can three times with three shots. "I'm better when I move," Sundance says, as he puts away his pistol.

Some students are better when they move. What would better demonstrate ability: Giving Joe Montana a written exam on how to win a Super Bowl, or giving him the ball with two minutes left in the Big Game? Some children just need to be given the ball. Too many children are asked to sit still for three hours to take a test or complete seat work. Essentially, schools are setting these students up for failure by asking them to perform a highly unnatural activity and behave in a way that is not developmentally appropriate. Allow these students to move around, interact with others, or complete a project-based activity, however, and these same students may prosper.

The purpose of schools is to teach. For students and teachers to learn, they need to be allowed to fail. Not everybody is good at everything, and this is why too many elementary school teachers leave the profession feeling they are failures. In fact, often they are excellent math teachers who need assistance teaching language arts. Sadly, too many teachers in today's educational climate are handcuffed by district mandates bent on boosting standardized test scores at all costs. If those costs include adding test preparation to the curricula at the expense of physical education, music, and time at the school library, so be it. Have the lunatics taken over the asylum? Activities like P.E. and music are precisely what students need more of if they are to prosper.

Thank goodness everyone is different, or society would be boring. We need to acknowledge our individual differences and focus on ways to utilize individuals' strengths. The way to boost students' esteem is to celebrate their uniqueness.

Provide Time for Practice

I love my mother. Growing up, whenever I asked her a question about my schoolwork that she could not answer, she would always claim that her family moved that semester, so she could not help me. Once I asked her for some assistance on Roman numerals, and Mom said, "I don't know Roman numerals. That was the year we moved." So the only reason I learned Roman numerals was because of the Super Bowl. And, sadly, I can only count up to around 46.

It is a shame that stressed-out teachers often cram a multitude of objectives into a brief time frame with little or no review. Imagine a teacher saying, "Sorry you missed school on Tuesday, Pablo. That was the day we learned how to add." Students need plenty of opportunities to practice and revisit skills. Good teachers facilitate these opportunities by providing lots of centers, projects, and questions that challenge and engage students.

If you are or have been a parent of a young child, you know that children will bring you the same book to read aloud every night. Why? Your child is memorizing that book. My daughter Kate would often ask me to read aloud *Balto* by Jane Mason (1995). It is the story of a stupid wolf-dog in Alaska. Now a lot of people plead with me, "You shouldn't say that; I like *Balto*." Try reading it 875 times, and we will see how much you enjoy it. Every night, my daughter would anxiously ask, "What's going to happen next?" I, of course, would feign complete surprise and claim, "I don't know, let's see." That is how you build confidence. Provide students plenty of time to learn routines and repeat them again and again.

Repetition is not a bad thing. Want to know why most veteran teachers are better teachers than beginning teachers? They have been doing it longer! Practice is important to master anything, which is another reason it is ridiculous to expect beginning teachers to be great teachers overnight. The repetition of working with different students builds confidence that is essential to any great teacher.

Here's a memory game you can play with students to demonstrate the importance of repetition. Show students a picture of a bed and ask them to listen carefully to a list of words: *dream, sleep, night, mattress, snooze, sheet, nod, tired, night, artichoke, insomnia, blanket, night, alarm, nap, snore,* and *pillow*. Pause for about 10 seconds and ask students to write down all the words that they can remember.

This game demonstrates four principles about memory. First, if students wrote down *dream* and *pillow*, they remembered the first and last words in the list. When people remember the first and last things in a series, this is known as the *primacy and recency effects*. The takeaway for teachers is to remember that the first and last items in a lesson tend to stick better than other parts, so pay careful attention to those parts of the lesson.

Second, most students will have written *night* because it was repeated three times. When people remember things that are repeated it is known as the *repetition effect*. Repetition is not a bad thing. The more we can expose students to a concept, the better.

Third, if students recalled the word *artichoke*, it is probably because that word is different from the other words. People tend to remember things that are novel or different. This is the *surprise effect*. What is the takeaway for teachers? Novelty is key. What are you doing to create a meaningful, unique moment for your students each day in class?

Finally, some students may have recalled the word *bed*. This is the *false memory effect*. The word *bed* was not on the list, but by showing students a picture of a bed and reading aloud words that are logically associated with a bed, some students will write the word *bed*. The brain closes logical gaps between what it hears, sees, or reads, frequently remembering things that did not take place. While context is key, we need to be careful, as teachers, not to confuse our students with too many materials.

The point of this activity is to demonstrate the value of context. The more context you can provide students through repeated exposure, the better. Repetition breeds confidence and familiarity and is a useful tool in mastering subject matter.

Check for Understanding

Have you ever noticed how at least half of Congress just nods at every statement that the president makes during his State of the Union address? Plenty of people do the same thing with their mechanic, as they hear him say, "Blah, blah, blah, blah, $375, blah, blah, blah."

People like surrounding themselves with agreeable people. Even in another country where you don't speak the language, you could converse with native speakers for hours simply by nodding and giggling occasionally.

What does all this mean to you? Do not fall into the "Does everybody understand?" trap. Chances are, students will simply nod their heads and say, "Yes." That does not mean they understand anything you are trying to explain.

Students need to *show* you that they understand. In the olden days, students wrote on slates and revealed their answers to the teacher. Rather than ask students if they understand, give each of them a small erasable board and ask them to write down what they just heard, saw, or solved. When they hold up their boards for you to inspect, you will have a clear picture of who really understands.

There are plenty of engaging ways to check for understanding. Get students out of their seats. One activity, known as "Four Corners," encourages students to walk to a particular corner of the room based on whether they agree, disagree, strongly agree, or strongly disagree with a statement. An easy way to prompt students to answer "yes or no" or "true or false" questions is to create a line in the classroom and ask students to walk to the side of the line that represents their opinion. If nothing else, a teacher can encourage students to use finger signals when answering questions (e.g., a fist in the air means the student does not know the answer; three fingers in the air means the student has an answer but may need help; five fingers raised means the student feels confident in her answer; and no hand in the air means the teacher will definitely call on the student). By incorporating movement, teachers can check for understanding and better involve all students.

Give Three Cheers for Tiers

Tiering is the heart of differentiation. A good classroom functions like a good high school athletics program. It has varsity, junior varsity, and freshman teams. Just because a student is not good enough to play on the varsity team does not mean the student should sit out the whole game. A good teacher can teach every standard in the curricula to every student. Some students meet the grade-level standard, while others exceed or fall below the standard. Teachers need to tier instruction as much as possible to meet the diverse needs of these students, as well as consider the added challenges for English language learners (ELLs).

With a little thought, almost anything in the classroom can be tiered. Many teachers find two to three tiers to be best for implementation, but a teacher who is experienced and comfortable with the strategy may have more tiers if it facilitates the instruction or better meets the needs of the students. Teachers can tier materials, assessments, assignments, activities, centers/stations, or homework. The teacher's challenge is to create a classroom that is interesting, challenging, and engaging for every student.

No student should look at a task and think, "I guess I'm in the dumb group." The key to developing effective tiered activities is to design them so they are just above the level of the learner. This helps every student stretch and build from where they are. Challenging and supporting students at their levels of understanding will help them to become successful learners. When tiering, teachers should consider making adjustments for students in different groups with materials, time and pacing, level of complexity, and amount of structure. The possibilities are only limited by the teacher's imagination.

 Compact the Curriculum

On the first day of a soccer practice, all of the players are asked to do the drills. But experienced players quickly show their mastery and want to learn new skills. The drills may serve as warm-ups, but the seasoned athletes are able to move on much more quickly than the novices.

Students compact or eliminate material which they have already mastered and move ahead to more challenging work. Some students already get it, and teachers recognize this when they see a student who always completes tasks quickly, finishes reading assignments first, appears bored during instruction time, daydreams, creates his or her own diversions in class, asks questions that indicate advanced familiarity with topics, and so forth.

Teachers "compact curriculum" (the process of identifying learning objectives, pre-testing students for prior mastery of these objects, and eliminating needless teaching practice if mastery can be documented [Reis and Purcell 1993]) to create more challenging learning environments for more advanced learners. It is important to note that while a student may be proficient in one area, he or she may not be so advanced in another. Again, teacher observation is critical in identifying students' readiness needs. Compacting allows teachers to assess what students already know and what they still need to master. It also allows teachers the opportunity to eliminate time spent on content that is already known so students can spend their time on more enriching activities.

Reflection Questions

1. What is a "souvenir" or other bit of realia that you can use tomorrow to capture your students' intellectual curiosity?

2. Make a list of stories you could share with your students. Are there ties you could make in the curriculum to these stories? Think of ways to integrate stories into your instruction.

3. It is easier to praise some students more than others— especially those who are eager to please and who work hard. Think of a student who is more of a challenge for you, perhaps someone quiet and unresponsive, or a student who pushes your buttons with his or her disruptive behavior. How could you offer that student specific and meaningful praise and have a positive impact on his or her self-esteem?

Self-Actualization Needs

Overview

Nobody should be allowed to tell a child what he or she can or cannot do. Potential is everywhere, and encouragement is sorely needed in schools. Pablo Picasso once said, "If there were only one truth, you couldn't paint a hundred canvases on the same theme." Wow! If you ever need a quote, go no further than Picasso. He constantly took risks and pursued his interests. He also had some pretty amazing thoughts about passion:

> *"If they took away my paints I'd use pastels. If they took away my pastels I'd use crayons. If they took away my crayons I'd use pencils. If they stripped me naked and threw me in prison I'd spit on my finger and paint on the walls."*

Dang! That guy liked to paint. He was not going to let anybody or anything stand between him and his passion. What a wonderful role model for children.

Maslow views the first four levels of needs as "deficit" needs: If you do not have enough of something, you feel the need. In contrast, if you get all you need, you feel nothing at all. In other words, once a need is met, it ceases to be motivating. For example, hunger is not a motivating factor once you've stuffed yourself with Thanksgiving dinner. Under stressful conditions, you can regress to a deficit need. For example, if your significant other leaves you, you may crave more love.

Maslow sees the first four levels of needs as essential needs. Even love and esteem are needed to maintain one's health. Maslow argues that we all have these needs built into us genetically—like instincts (1954).

At the summit of Maslow's Hierarchy is what he calls "self-actualization." To reach this summit, all of your deficit needs must be met. Self-actualization needs involve the continuous desire to fulfill potentials. George Bernard Shaw put it this way: "Some look at things that are and ask why. I dream of things that never were and ask why not?"

Self-actualization is the ultimate pathway to joy in the classroom. In the joyful classroom, the journey is just as important as the destination. When you reach this level of Maslow's Hierarchy, you are within the realm of possibilities rather than the realm of scarcities. You are creative and original, as well as humble, and you do not take yourself too seriously in the joyful classroom. You reach your true potential—the ultimate goal!

Buckminster Fuller once said that "all children are born geniuses, and we spend the first six years of their lives de-geniusing them" (1994). Too often schools revolve around scripted programs and drill-and-kill practice instead of focusing on children's interests and learning styles. Too often teachers abandon their own interests and desires and conform. Once they relent, their passion and joy slowly erode.

Ever see a person with a "mullet"? A mullet is a hair cut (usually on men) that is short in the front and on the sides but long in the back. The way one talk show host used to describe the mullet was "business in front and a party in the back." A joyful classroom is sort of like a mullet in reverse: Party in the front and business in the back.

Teachers have a ton of standards to teach, especially in an age where "no child is left untested" and everybody is "racing to cheat to get to the top." Have you ever noticed that if everyone is racing to the top, plenty of people are going to be left behind? In school districts around the country, national education accountability has become more urgent. In essence, school districts keep pushing skills to lower and lower grade levels in order to accommodate the growing list of skills the schools are expected to teach. Plenty of standards keep getting added, and nothing is taken away. Have you seen skills that fifth grade teachers used to teach now being introduced in second grade? While lots of educators are shouting about the overwhelming research promoting developmental appropriateness, policy makers feel the heat to boost test scores. The result is a lot of miserable students and embittered teachers.

No! That's not for you. It is time to rise up and bring the joy back into classrooms! Great teachers focus on great teaching. Great teachers consistently feed their students educational medicine by disguising it as a treat.

Good teachers offer plenty of activities to allow students to make sense of or understand information, ideas, and skills being studied in different ways. These activities reflect student learning styles and preferences and vary depending upon how students learn. The activities should be so appealing to students that they do not even realize that they are learning. True learning is effortless because students enjoy it so much.

Differentiated classrooms offer students tasks that encourage them to think at high levels. Good teachers provide all students with consistent opportunities to be active learners, working with a wide variety of peers over time. Students in these classrooms are constantly challenged by taking a greater stake in their learning, teaching their peers, and designing their own activities.

So what does it mean to help students reach their full potential?

Quick Strategies for Promoting Self-Actualization

1. **Be flexible.** Set up stations in the classroom where different learners can work simultaneously on various tasks. Such stations naturally invite flexible grouping (meaning some students work in small groups, others work with partners, and still others may opt to work alone).

2. **Give them ownership.** Let students create the agenda—personalized lists of tasks that each student must complete in a specified time, usually two to three weeks. Agendas can be personalized for individual students or for group tasks. Students work individually or in groups to complete the agenda tasks.

3. **Make it concrete.** Provide students with (and model the use of) planning think-sheets, graphic organizers, concept maps, story maps, or study guides to support reading and writing activities.

4. **Set them free.** Allow students opportunities to work independently to investigate topics of interest to them. Students spend a lot more time learning material in authentic, meaningful ways that bring them joy when they are actually engaged. In addition, by freeing students to pursue activities that attract their own interests, teachers can devote more time to working with individuals who may be struggling.

5. **Provide options.** Use choice boards (some teachers call these "menus" of options) that allow students to select one of several assignments, on a particular topic, that are printed on cards and affixed to the choice boards. To ensure students pursue different activities, teachers can ask students to perform a combination of activities. For example, one fourth grade teacher teaching students about inventors told them that they needed 30 points to complete the unit on inventors. Then she provided students six options for earning points, varying from 20-point activities like writing biographies on inventors to 5-point activities like creating comic strips about inventors. No matter which options students chose, they needed to combine different activities in order to earn full credit (so they could choose a 20-point activity and a 10-point activity or six different 5-point activities, if they wanted).

6. **Engage and activate their curiosity.** Motivate your students to explore topics in greater depth by creating plenty of high-interest centers or workstations. These centers/workstations are classroom areas that contain a collection of activities or materials designed to teach, reinforce, or extend a particular skill or concept, classified by students' interests and profiles of learning. Everything can become a center. For example, after reading aloud a Shel Silverstein poem to students, you could place the poem in the "Shel Center" and offer students the chance to rewrite the poem using characters and settings from the class, write a new stanza to the poem, turn the poem from a limerick to an acrostic, and so forth.

7. **Introduce the element of chance.** Prepare 12 cards that will comprise two "cubes" with different activities for demonstrating understanding of any subject. This activity appeals to different learning styles. Students select a method of sharing and showing understanding of a topic with classmates by rolling the paper cubes and choosing one of the activities that appear face up on the cube. The student then produces the activity and shares it with the class. Simply introducing the element of chance is often a way to entice students' interests.

8. **Encourage accountability.** Use small, individual marker boards to check for student understanding. The process requires participation from all students, not just those likely to participate in class discussions, as they must use their boards to demonstrate their participation and understanding.

9. **Partner up.** Use the "clock buddy" strategy when you want to pair students for discussion or review. Students receive a handout of a clock and write a classmate's name for each hour on the clock. When they find a partner for a certain hour, each buddy must record the other's name on the clock. Students cannot partner with the same person

until they have gone through all of the "hours" of their clocks. This is also a great way to encourage students to interact with a variety of classmates rather than with the same three kids.

10. **Keep them guessing.** Use craft sticks to encourage all students to be active listeners and participate in class discussions. Write each student's name on a craft stick and place the sticks in a container at the front of the room. When holding a class discussion, randomly draw a stick. The person named on the stick responds to the question. Make sure that you replace the student's stick back in the container so they realize that they can be called upon again; that way, they know they have to pay attention.

11. **Practice writing.** Give students the task of writing a summary of a problem in 12 words or less. Another good activity is to ask students to write "six-word stories." There is a great website, http://www.sixwordstories.net, that requires writers to write stories that are only six words long. Students quickly discover that it is not always easy to be succinct. Twitter is another good way to promote precision in writing, as the service only allows writers to convey a point in 144 characters or less.

12. **Prepare for downtime.** Provide students with lists of anchoring activities that they can do at any time throughout the day when they have completed their assignments. These activities may relate to specific needs or enrichment opportunities, including problems to solve or journal topics to write. They could also be part of a long-term project that a student is working on. The use of these activities may allow the teacher time to provide specific assistance and small-group instruction to students requiring additional help on the present assignment. When all else fails, teachers can provide "book bins" at tables where students can grab a book to read for pleasure as a reward for finishing an activity early. Of course, the best downtime activity is reading for fun!

13. **Give students mystery tasks.** Almost everyone loves a mystery. A good way to lure students into a topic is to wrap it in a puzzle or detective story. This works well at the elementary school level, but can also be extended all the way up to adult learners.

14. **Make mental maps.** Ask students to visually map key elements that derive from new vocabulary, using the 3-2-1 technique. Students first describe three facts that they discovered, then they write down two interesting things they would want to share, and finally, one question that they still have.

15. **Establish bonds.** Encourage students to collaborate through buddy-studies. A buddy-study permits two or three students to work together on a project. The expectation is that all may share the research and analysis or organization of information, but each student must complete an individual product to demonstrate learning that has taken place and be accountable for his or her own planning, time management, and individual accomplishment.

Fifteen Ways to Meet Your Self-Actualization Needs

 Think Big

A woman steps into an elevator and tells the operator to take her to the 11th floor. The elevator operator asks, "Whom do you wish to see on the 11th floor?" The woman snaps back, "That's none of your business." The operator apologizes and says, "I'm not being nosy. It's just that this building only has eight floors."

You need to "think big." However, there is a difference between thinking big and setting unrealistic expectations. Some policy makers insist that 100 percent of students should meet prescribed mathematics and reading proficiency levels by this year or that. Then they don't provide enough supplementary funding to make that happen. The real question is not whether something is possible; the real question is whether you are willing to take the necessary steps to accomplish that goal.

A professor prepared a test for his soon-to-be-graduating students. The test questions were divided into three categories, and the test instructed students to choose questions from only one of the categories. The first category of questions was the hardest and worth 50 points. The second—which happened to be easier—was worth 40 points. The third—the simplest—was worth 30 points. Upon completion of the test, students who had chosen the hardest 50-point questions received As, those choosing the 40-point questions earned Bs, and those who settled for the easiest 30-pointers were given Cs. Frustrated students complained to the professor and asked what he was looking for. The professor leaned over the podium and smiled. "I wasn't testing your knowledge," he explained. "I was testing your goals."

Henry Ford said, "Whether you believe you can do a thing or not, you are right." Your students will achieve precisely what you think they will achieve. You will achieve precisely what you think you can achieve. If you want to achieve big things, you need to think big. Why settle? Striving to meet district benchmarks is all fine and good, but why not strive to guide students even further in one year, so that movie studios are clamoring to film movies about your class? Incorporate that philosophy into your classroom, and you will be dazzled by what your students can accomplish.

Enjoy the Journey

We know the ends do not necessarily justify the means. But means can be ends themselves, since the journey is often more important than the destination. Stop and enjoy your students, your class, and your colleagues.

Ask yourself, "Does it get any better than this?" If the answer is "yes," then why not start making it better?

Do you want the secret of ensuring joy in your classroom every day? Love what you do. Gordon Livingston (2006) points out that most illnesses are psychosomatic. People literally think themselves into sicknesses. He provides some tips to "the over-65 bunch" that should be heeded by educators of all ages:

1. Stop complaining. A couple of generations ago, you would have been dead for 10 years.

2. If you don't have an activity in your life that causes you to lose track of time, you need to find one.

3. If you go to the doctor more than 10 times a year and don't have a terminal illness, get a hobby.

4. It's true that they haven't written any good music for 30 years. Neither your children nor your grandchildren want to hear about it.

5. If anyone wants to know what life was like when you were their age, they'll ask.

6. Don't worry about avoiding temptation. As you grow older, it will avoid you.

7. Never mind dying with dignity; try living with dignity.

Have you ever seen *The Shawshank Redemption* (1994)? If you have not, rent a copy right away. Andy (played by Tim Robbins) challenges his friend, Red (played by Morgan Freeman), to get busy living or get busy dying. Red chooses to get busy living. Have you taught with any teachers who complain about their low pay, lack of respect, low benefits, sore backs, and so on, and so on? These are the folks who talk themselves into misery each and every day. On the opposite end of the spectrum, have you taught with extraordinary teachers who laugh about the silliness of a particular child or who relish the incredible improvement of a student whom others had neglected? These teachers, like Red, are choosing to get busy living. Even Donald Trump (who has had his share of financial missteps), when asked what was the secret to happiness, said, "Love what you do, and never give up."

 ## Take Thought Walks

Professional athletes have a huge advantage over most people. After they play a game, journalists thrust microphones into their faces and ask them to review their performances. What a great exercise in reflection. Good teachers reflect on their practices constantly. One great way to relax the mind and focus is by taking "thought walks" on the beach. You may not have a beach near you, but anyone can take a walk, breathe fresh air, and pause to reflect on his or her teaching practices.

Teachers should take the opportunity to think aloud, discuss their thinking with their peers, and reflect on their thinking in journals in order to inform their own teaching. For example, if you teach a lesson plan that bombs, do you quit your job, become an alcoholic and start talking to trash dumpsters? Hopefully, the answer is "no," especially since students need to see you flop from time to time. Try not to worry about it, since students are some of the most forgiving audiences. What failed today should help you to do better tomorrow.

Students need the same opportunity to reflect. Ask students to discuss their learning strategies openly so they can affirm or compare other strategies with their own methods. Have you ever had a student complain that he had studied for a final exam for two entire days and wound up failing? Ignore the temptation to issue a sarcastic response, and instead suggest that he should change his study strategies. Perhaps next time he should study alone, without the television turned on, and without talking on the phone. Some students study better when they work with a partner. Putting some students together, however, is like reinventing TNT. Students need to reflect on what works. More importantly, when they find something that works, they should stick to that strategy.

 ## Seek Depth, Not Breadth

What sounds more appealing: mastering one thing or being mediocre at many things? Focus on what you do well, and do that thing all of the time.

Winston Lloyd was an aide to Secretary of State Henry Kissinger. One day Lloyd brought Kissinger a long-awaited report on conflicts in South America. Without even glancing at the report, Kissinger asked, "Is this the very best you can do?" Lloyd stammered for a few moments and said, "There were a few informational gaps." "Take it back," Kissinger said and dismissed him. Two weeks later, after working night and day, Lloyd again entered Kissinger's office and held out the report. "Is this the very best you can do?" Kissinger asked, without looking at the document. Lloyd hesitated and admitted there were some parts of the report that were incomplete. Kissinger told him to take it back. Three weeks later, Lloyd asked for another meeting. For the third time Kissinger asked, "Is this the very best you can do?" Lloyd replied, "Mr. Secretary, this is my very best effort." Kissinger smiled and said, "That's all I ever ask. I'll be happy to read your report."

In today's classrooms, many teachers are required to cover so many standards that they have little time to explore topics in depth. How can anyone develop a love of learning at such a superficial level? Think about your favorite foods, activities, or people. How many of these did you grow a deeper fondness for over time and repeated exposure? Why should school be any different?

Students should actually understand the information teachers present. Who cares if it takes 87 reviews before some students get it? What is the point in moving on if a student does not grasp something? They say patience is a virtue. Patience is essential in great teaching. If it takes 87 different strategies to help a student grasp a concept, that student just helped his teacher learn a lot of new ways to approach a problem. One common characteristic of poor teaching is looking at student difficulties as impediments. Great teachers view student difficulties as opportunities. Take the time to dive deeper into a topic to make it more meaningful to your students. You may be surprised by how much more they learn and retain.

Don't Worry, Be Happy

In one of Charles Schultz's many *Peanuts*® cartoons, Lucy asks Charlie Brown if he has ever known anybody who was really happy. Before she can finish her sentence, however, Snoopy comes dancing on his tiptoes into the picture, his nose high in the air. He dances and bounces his way across two frames of the cartoon strip. Finally, in the last frame, Lucy finishes her sentence: "Have you ever known anybody who was really happy…and was still in his right mind?"

Americans love happy endings. Just look at American films. Hollywood producer Sam Goldwyn once listened to director Billy Wilder describe in detail the true-life story of a famous artist. Goldwyn thought it would make a great movie and asked if it had a happy ending. "Well," Wilder said, "it winds up with the guy in an insane asylum thinking he's a horse." Goldwyn threw Wilder out the door. A few moments later, Wilder poked his head back in. "Okay," he said. "How about if at the end, the guy who thinks he's a horse…goes on to win the Kentucky Derby?"

While so much emphasis is placed on students' test scores, perhaps there is another way to measure how students are doing in school: by their happiness. Think that's crazy? In 1972, Bhutan's economy, measured by its Gross National Product (GNP), was growing poorly. So King Jigme Singye Wangchuck decided to define his country's quality of life in more holistic and psychological terms by measuring his country's well-being and happiness using an indicator he deemed Gross National Happiness (GNH). The king argued that subjective measures like well-being are more relevant and important than more objective measures like consumption. Wouldn't it be nice to measure students not solely by what they take away from your classroom, but also by what they give back to the world? Happiness is not a waste of time; it is a noble goal for any teacher.

 Laugh at Yourself

Keep a notebook in your desk to write down all of the silly things that happen in your classroom. I once led a social studies lesson where I asked a boy, Sergio, to point to the United States on a map. Then I asked the class who discovered America, and all of my students responded, "Sergio."

Leave your pride at the door. Learn to laugh at yourself. One of the best ways to promote joy in your classroom is to keep everybody in check—don't let anyone take himself or herself too seriously.

Have you ever misspelled a word on the board? Inevitably, some student will point out your mistake. That's ok. Just smile and say, "This is a game we're going to play all year long. I am going to intentionally misspell words from time to time to see if you are paying attention."

You set the tone for everything in your classroom. If you take yourself too seriously, your students will follow. Human beings are more approachable when their flaws are out in the open for all to see. A little laughter, especially at one's own expense, is a great way of building classroom unity. It is also a great way to remind yourself why you love what you do.

 Be Fair

What is intelligence? What does it mean? Most schools have a definition of what they believe students need to know. This is what guides their curriculum. Yet students bring diverse backgrounds and styles of learning that, when recognized, can greatly assist them in soaring to new heights.

Matching learning opportunities to learning profiles maximizes efficiency and effectiveness of learning for individuals. Everyone benefits when his or her needs are met. Before teachers can differentiate instruction, they must understand the ideal learning conditions of their students by looking for different ways to determine various students' "points of entry" into topics and skills, what individual students gravitate towards both in and out of school, and the sorts of learning environments and conditions in which various students will succeed. Teachers do this through ongoing assessment—which no longer means tests and quizzes at the end of a unit. Assessment is a teacher's continual examination of students' learning profiles for the purpose of better understanding today how to modify tomorrow's instruction.

Howard Gardner (2006) said, "The biggest mistake of past centuries in teaching has been to treat all children as if they were variants of the same individual, and thus to feel justified in teaching them all the same subjects in the same way." One of the most important researchers of the last 50 years, Gardner developed his Multiple Intelligence Theory, which amounts to what I call a "Gary Coleman" approach to teaching: different strokes for different folks. All students are different, and this is the challenge teachers confront every day. For some teachers, this may be a daunting challenge. To others, recognizing student differences and accommodating instruction to suit students' needs is the joy of teaching.

Students do not need to be treated equally. Equality is overrated in this country. Students need to be treated fairly, as some students only require a nudge, while others require an all-out shove. Your responsibility as a teacher is to be equitable by giving each student what he or she needs. Teaching all students the same way is like handing out Rocky Road ice cream to everyone: some may be thrilled, but others may not care for it.

Over the past 20 years or so, there has been a debate in higher education about how best to teach students to read. Some advocates insist on drilling students daily on sounds that would annoy a crow, such as "Aaa...aaa...alligator, bbb...bbb...ball, ccc...ccc...cat!" That's the way we all "sss...sss...speak," right? And then you see teachers who light their aroma candles and peacefully ask students to take their books home, put them under their pillows and pray that when they wake up they will know how to read. Of course, great teachers recognize that it is helpful for students to understand the sounds of letters and to have opportunities for free reading. However, have you observed that if a child loves filling out phonics worksheets, you should give that student phonics worksheets? Or, if a child loves reading in the corner alone, you should allow it? The school was built for them, not for you. Your job as a teacher is to identify how students learn best and design programs of instruction that build on these strengths.

⇒ Keep It Simple

Have you ever seen the movie *The Dirty Dozen* (1967)? There is one particular scene in the film that teachers should heed. Lee Marvin leads a bunch of misfits on a secret mission. In order for his "dirty dozen" to remember their assignments, he leads the group in a recitation of their attack:

> "One—down at the roadblock, we've just begun. Two—the guards are through! Three—the Major's men are on a spree! Four—the Major and Wladislaw go through the door! Five—Pinkley stays out in the drive. Six—the Major gives the rope a fix. Seven—Wladislaw throws the hook to heaven. Eight—Jiminez has a date. Nine—the other guys go up the line. Ten—Sawyer and Gilpen are in the pen. Eleven—Posey guards points 5 and 7. Twelve—Wladislaw and the Major go down to delve."

Lee Marvin is dealt a ragged bunch of men, upon whom everyone else in the Army has given up, but Lee Marvin knows that his life and all of their lives are at stake on this mission. His job is to do whatever it takes to get his dirty dozen to work together on a common mission. He makes the content of the mission accessible to the entire platoon by creating a simple rhyme that he reviews ad nauseam with his soldiers. In this way, he has taken a complicated plan and made it understandable to his men. This is what good teachers do every day with their curricula and—like Lee Marvin—they find greater satisfaction in their trade.

Jigsaw puzzles are a lot easier to solve when you see the whole picture first. The same proves true for all content in classrooms. Students can have a much easier time developing their understandings of particular items when they see the "big picture" first.

Have you ever seen the (original) movie *The Karate Kid* (1984)? Is Mr. Miyagi really such a great teacher? In the film, Daniel (played by Ralph Macchio) is bullied, and he seeks the karate teachings of his building's superintendent and handyman, Mr. Miyagi (played by Academy Award nominee Pat Morita). Mr. Miyagi trains "Daniel-*sahn*" by enlisting the boy to do all of his housework, from painting fences to waxing cars. Daniel-*sahn* eventually becomes fed up and confronts Mr. Miyagi. Daniel protests that he is sick of being a slave.

Mr. Miyagi looks him over and asks, "Show me, 'wax on, wax off.'" Daniel-*sahn* half-heartedly demonstrates to Mr. Miyagi how he waxed the cars, when Mr. Miyagi stops him and shouts, "No! Wax on! Wax off!" And he demonstrates to Daniel-*sahn* how the repetitive movements of waxing a car are the same movements he needs to master karate. At that point, Daniel-*sahn* has an epiphany. "Oh," he thinks. "I was learning karate." If Mr. Miyagi was a good teacher, before he forced Daniel to do all his chores, he could have mentioned, "By the way, kid, the repetitive motions you'll be practicing doing these chores are the same ones you need to master karate."

How many teachers dive into sub-skills with students without ever mentioning how these activities fit into the big picture? It is possible that half of the kindergartners in the United States have no idea why they are there. Their heads bob like jelly as they scan their classrooms asking themselves, "What's going on? I was just dropped off here one day." Good teachers explain the purpose of their activities. They explain the "method to their madness," so to speak. They keep things simple so students progress from one level to the next without stress.

Stay Humble, Don't Grumble

President Lyndon Johnson once asked his press secretary, Bill Moyers (who was also a minister), to offer the mealtime prayer. Moyers began by praying quietly. President Johnson became somewhat irritated. "Pray louder!" he interrupted. Moyers looked up and replied, "I'm sorry, sir, but I wasn't addressing you."

It is important to keep your ego in check. Being humble puts people in their proper place. Nobody is better than anyone else. Just when a teacher thinks she knows something, a student sets her straight. Have you ever had a child point out the obvious? It seems adults often fail to pay attention to children, even though children make valid points. One of the reasons Art Linkletter enjoyed so much success with his books and show, *Kids Say the Darndest Things* is because children often see things in a very different (and often more logical) way than adults.

A journalism professor once gave a pop quiz. The last question read, "What is the first name of the man who cleans this building?" After the test, the professor said that the question counted for half of the grade. Despite the protests of his students, the professor just shook his head. "In your careers you will meet many people. All are significant, and they deserve your attention and care, even if all you do is smile and say hello." Make it a point to introduce yourself to everyone in the building. You never know where that connection can lead.

Make Things Better

In 1994, golfer Davis Love III called a one-stroke penalty on himself during the second round of the Western Open. He had moved his marker on a green to get it out of another player's putting line. One or two holes later, he couldn't remember if he had moved his ball back to its original spot. Unsure, Love gave himself an extra stroke.

As it turned out, that one stroke caused him to miss the cut and get knocked out of the tournament. If he had made the cut and then finished dead last, he would have earned $2,000 for the week. When the year was over, Love fell $590 short of automatically qualifying for the following year's Masters Golf Tournament. Love began 1995 needing to win a tournament to get into the event. When someone asked how much it would bother him if he missed the Masters for calling a penalty on himself, Love's answer was simple: "How would I feel if I won the Masters and wondered for the rest of my life if I cheated to get in?"

Character and integrity are dwindling natural resources. Your students watch everything you do, and that is a tremendous responsibility that every teacher must take very seriously. All teachers are in the position to mold students.

Your job as a teacher is to make students better people, not just smarter people. Teaching young children, in particular, can give you a better perspective on what is important. Remind students they do not have to be the next "American Idol" to make a difference. All they really need to learn is how to say "please" and "thank you," hold the door open for others, and tell their parents "I love you." It is the little things that people do that matter the most. What kind of people do you want to mold your students to become?

By the way, the week before the 1995 Masters, Davis Love managed to qualify by winning a tournament in New Orleans. In the Masters, he finished in second place, earning $237,600. More often than we hear about, nice guys do finish first.

Make Every Day Your Masterpiece

Ron Newhouse (http://www.devotions.net) writes a story about a girl recalling an incident with her grandmother that happened when the girl was about 10 years old:

> "Grandma received a gift of perfume in a bottle that fascinated me. Made of green pottery with a long, slender neck and square bottom, it looked like pictures I had seen of ancient ware. I begged Grandma to open it. 'No,' she said. 'I'm going to save it until later.' When I was 33, Grandma gave [the perfume] to me saying, 'Let's see how long you can keep it without opening it.'"

> "One day when I picked up the perfume bottle, I was shocked to discover that it was empty, although still sealed. Turning it over, I could see why. The bottom of the bottle had never been glazed. The perfume had slowly evaporated through the porous clay. How sad that no one ever enjoyed the perfume—not Grandma or anyone else!"

What are you waiting for? If you are waiting for others to make you happy, you are in for a long wait. Instead of waiting for others to compliment you, why not try complimenting others? Make every day your masterpiece, and constantly encourage your students.

Marcel Proust said, "The real art of discovery consists not in finding new lands, but in seeing with new eyes." The more teachers try to see their classrooms through the eyes of their students, the better they can serve their students' needs. Encourage students to take risks and make mistakes every day.

Gordon MacKenzie (1998) conducted a wonderful study where he went into different elementary classrooms and asked students how many of them were artists. In the first grade classrooms he visited, students leapt from their seats waving their hands—all of them were artists. In the second grade classrooms he observed, about half the kids raised their hands while sitting in their seats, and their arms were still. In the third grade classrooms, about a third of the students raised their hands, shoulder high. By the time he reached the sixth grade classrooms, MacKenzie observed that only one or two students raised their hands, and with quite a bit of trepidation. The point is, MacKenzie confirms something that is prevalent in too many schools: Students are often discouraged from taking risks, which impacts them for years to come.

That is a crime. The job of teachers is to encourage as much creativity and input from students as possible. Everyone, hopefully, learns from mistakes.

As creativity expert Ken Robinson (2009) points out, "If you're not prepared to be wrong, you will never come up with anything original."

 ## Be an Original

The only way teachers can succeed is to ensure that all students are working together toward the same goal of continuous growth and improvement. Complacency is a prescription for failure. Teachers need to constantly challenge themselves and their students to reach higher, and this is made so much easier with the support of peers and superiors.

Here is a controversial idea for you: Give each of your students an A. There are two reasons you should try this. First, have you considered the consequences for the student if he or she comes home with a failing grade? Second, look at the research. Where in the research does it show that a letter grade reflects what a student learns? We've all had classes as children where we goofed off but still earned an A because we completed the "extra credit." And we've all had other classes where we worked our hardest only to earn a C, and yet we learned more in those classes than any others.

Congress is a perfect example of this concept. Congress illustrates that you do not have to be the sharpest tool in the shed to succeed in the United States. There is something that Congress does, however, that the research does support: They show up. It seems ludicrous that so many folks are fixated on grading and labeling students in this country. Attendance is much more important, since "the research" shows that students who show up to school perform much better than students who skip. Any administrator will readily admit that attendance is crucial, because most public schools receive funding based on attendance. Educators' top priority is to inspire students to fill those seats every day not because of money (although that does not hurt), but because they will learn so much more through regular attendance and participation in school.

 ## Seek Peaks

People who experience self-actualization tend to have more "peak" experiences. A peak experience is one that takes you out of yourself. Think of a time when you taught and everything worked: Students laughed at the right moments, everyone understood the explanations and everyone eagerly participated. How do you recreate that on a daily basis?

Too many people focus on their problems. The very act of focusing on the problem contributes to the problem. Focus on solutions. Athletes understand this. Many pay big bucks to psychologists to help them develop a winning mindset. After winning the Masters, golfer Mike Weir explained he was in a zone and could literally visualize the ball rolling in the hole. On the other hand, plenty of golfers have played rounds of golf where they thought, "I hope I don't hit it into that water hazard." Guess what? They tend to hit the ball into the water hazard because they focused on it.

True joy comes from putting forth your best effort. Basketball legend Bill Russell said that some of the greatest games he played were those where the level of play was so high that he did not even care who won. More than once there have been Olympic athletes who do not win a medal but joyfully proclaim, "That was the best performance I ever had!" Focusing on one's process is the key to self-actualization. The product is secondary when you are satisfied with your effort. People who put forth their best effort never fail. The only one who can define that effort, though, is you.

 Practice

Gary Player won more international golf tournaments in his day than anyone else. When Player competed in tournaments, people constantly approached him and made the same remark: "I'd give anything if I could hit a golf ball like you." One particularly tough day, a tired and frustrated Player once again heard the tired refrain: "I'd give anything if I could hit a golf ball like you." Player's usual politeness failed him. "No, you wouldn't," he told the spectator. "You'd give anything to hit a golf ball like me if it was easy." Player took a deep breath and continued: "Do you know what you've got to do to hit a golf ball like me? You've got to get up at five o'clock in the morning, go out on the course, and hit one thousand golf balls. Your hand starts bleeding, and you walk up to the clubhouse, wash the blood off your hand, slap a bandage on it, and go out and hit another one thousand golf balls. That's what it takes to hit a golf ball like me."

Anyone can teach. But it takes a lot of hard work and practice to be a great teacher. Rafe Esquith teaches fifth grade at Hobart Elementary in South Los Angeles. He is at school from 6:00 A.M. to 6:00 P.M. six days a week, and he spends his vacations taking students on field trips all over the country. He is so committed to what he does, a lot of people think he should be committed. But Esquith's motto is, "There are no shortcuts." He models that every day.

If you really want to be good at anything, you have to practice, practice, practice. My daughter Kate's kindergarten teacher sent home leveled books as homework. Each book became more difficult than its predecessor. Kate enjoyed reading the books when they were easier, but she grew frustrated as the levels advanced. When Kate complained how hard the books were becoming, I told her that anything worth doing takes a lot of practice, and I pointed out to her how much she had improved. Nobody likes to practice, I assured her, but nobody gets any better at any activity without practicing.

To teachers everywhere, remember: Tomorrow is a new day. You will be better tomorrow than you were today. Stick with it. Practice is the only way to improve.

 Set Solid Goals

During the darkest days of the Civil War, President Abraham Lincoln had to sustain the hopes of the Union. When a delegation called at the White House to catalogue the crises facing America, Lincoln comforted them with a story. "Years ago," he said, "a young friend and I were out one night when a shower of meteors fell from the clear November sky. The young man was frightened, but I told him to look up in the sky past the shooting stars to the fixed stars beyond, shining serene in the firmament, and I said, 'Let us not mind the meteors, but let us keep our eyes on the stars.'"

Your students come to you with varying readiness levels, interests, and learning styles. Carol Ann Tomlinson, Howard Gardner, Mel Levine and many others have made significant contributions to education by forcing educators to acknowledge differences among students. Whether you work with high school students, middle school students, upper elementary school students, or very young students, they generally progress at similar rates. The big factor a lot of people want to ignore is that some students enter school at a very low level, while others enter at a very high level. That gap is a major hindrance to some students' education.

You have a choice to make every day. Do you moan about how tough your job is, or celebrate the challenges in your class? In legendary UCLA basketball coach John Wooden's remarkable book, *They Call Me Coach* (2004), Wooden lists the best coaches he has observed. The obvious choices would have been coaches who had more wins and titles than all others, but Wooden chose to select coaches who got the maximum effort out of their players. While some of these coaches did not have as high a winning percentage as others, Wooden noted, their teams managed to come closer to their own particular ability levels than any national championship teams that he had observed. Wooden judged coaches for their teaching abilities and for developing well-rounded student athletes who played nearest to their full potentials.

There is a remarkable bestselling book that says people should treat others the way they want to be treated. If you do not want to be treated like an imbecile, do not treat other people like imbeciles. Value and respect the abilities, talents, and interests of all of your students, and expect all of them to excel throughout the course of your time together. If they do not progress, it means you are not giving them what they need. Teachers can complain about the students that they have in their classrooms, or celebrate the opportunities and challenges that present themselves through their students. You must constantly strive to improve in an attempt to meet your full potential. Failing to prepare new goals is, as coach Wooden put it, preparing to fail.

Just like Abraham Lincoln's advice, why focus on the trouble spots in your life? Those are the meteors, fleeting and not long-lasting. Look at what endures in your class. Hopefully, it's the joy.

Reflection Questions

1. Do you love what you do? How do you show that joy to your students?

2. Are you consistently reminding your students about the "big picture"? Think of the lessons you just finished teaching. Did your students know how those concepts fit into the bigger picture?

3. Think about a recent moment of self-actualization you experienced. How could you replicate that situation?

CHAPTER 7

Conclusion

Do you want to feel joy in your classroom? Keep a journal handy in your desk to record all of the funny things you experience every day. In this book I have shared plenty of personal anecdotes from my own classroom. Some of my favorite anecdotes have come from educators throughout America:

- A fifth grader left his teacher a note that read, "Dear Ms. A., You are my favorite teacher. You are kind and patient. You are the most beautiful person I know. Love, Mark." Then the teacher read her student's scribbled postscript. "P. S. I don't know many people."

- A second grade teacher asked a student why she was doing her math multiplication on the floor. The student replied, "Because you told me to do it without using tables."

- A first grade teacher spent countless hours administering DIBELS® tests to her 23 students. After giving one girl a series of letter and letter-sound recognition tests, the student was asked to identify some "nonsense" words. After identifying a few such words, the girl asked the teacher why she was doing this. The teacher said she was testing students to see if they knew all the sounds and could blend them together as words. The girl frowned and said, "These are not words. These are dumb." Then she told her teacher she already knew how to read, and she got up to find a book in the classroom library. The teacher confessed that she agreed with the girl, and she decided to spend the rest of the day reading "real" words with her students.

- When a kindergarten teacher asked her class to recite the four seasons, one boy proudly proclaimed, "Salt, pepper, mustard, and vinegar!"

- A first grade teacher asked a student to give her a sentence starting with "I." The girl began, "I is," when the teacher interrupted to tell her, "No, always begin a sentence with '*I* am.'" The little girl looked perplexed and said, "*I* am the letter after '*H*.'"

Keep funny anecdotes handy. They will bring a smile to your face and remind you that no matter how hard it may seem, there is always a way to find joy in your classroom. Maybe you'll find joy in a child's silly comment, a colleague's struggles with a certain student or your own inability to teach a certain standard. It may take a while, but you can learn to loosen up and stop taking yourself so darn seriously. (To share your own funny anecdotes from your classroom, please email me via my website at http://www.dannybrassell.com.)

I am a teacher. I love what I do. It is not easy, which is precisely what makes it so rewarding. I choose to learn every day. I yearn to inspire and excite my students. It is both thrilling and terrifying to me that I am empowered to mold the lives of so many. I used to question if I was qualified to handle such a challenge before I realized many more qualified candidates failed to take the challenge. I put forth my best effort, and I am proud of what I do.

Look in the mirror. Are you a teacher? Smile, tap your shoes three times, and realize that you are living the dream, and that so many others' dreams depend on you.

Thank you for all that you do, and never forget how important you are. Never forget to smile. Never forget to laugh and dance and sing and color. Never forget to bring joy back into your classroom!

Reflection Questions

1. What is the funniest thing that happened this week? Start a journal today! Keep a running list of anecdotes.

2. What are you thankful for? Write down one thing you are grateful for every day. At the end of the year, go back and reread your journal. You may be surprised at what a great year you had!

3. What is one way you will bring joy into your classroom tomorrow?

References

Akaaboune, M., Culican, S. M., Turney, S. G., and Lichtman, J. W. 1999. Rapid and reversible effects of activity on acetylcholine receptor density at the neuromuscular junction in vivo. *Science*: 503–507.

Andrade, J. 2010. What does doodling do? *Applied Cognitive Psychology* 24 (1):100–106.

Blanchard, K. and B. Glanz. 2005. *The simple truths of service.* Naperville, IL: Simple Truths.

Blanchard, K. and S. Johnson. 1982. *The one-minute manager.* New York: HarperCollins Publishers, Inc.

Brafman, O. and R. Brafman. 2008. *Sway: The irresistible pull of irrational behavior.* New York: Broadway Books.

Brassell, D. 2009. *75+ reading strategies: Boost achievement and build a life-long love of reading.* Peterborough, NH: Crystal Springs Books.

———. 2009. *A baker's dozen of lessons learned from the teaching trenches.* Huntington Beach, CA: Shell Education.

Brassell, D. and T. Rasinski. 2008. *Comprehension that works: Taking students beyond ordinary understanding.* Huntington Beach, CA: Shell Education.

Bronson, P. 2002. *What should I do with my life?* New York: Random House.

Conklin, W. 2007. *Applying differentiation strategies.* Huntington Beach, CA: Shell.

Croce, P. 2000. *I feel great and you will too!* Philadelphia, PA: Running Press.

Diamond, M. and J. L. Hopson. 1998. *The magic trees of the mind: How to nurture your child's intelligence, creativity, and healthy emotions from birth through adolescence.* New York: Penguin Putnam, Inc.

Drucker, P. 2007. *Innovation and entrepreneurship* (2nd ed.). Portsmouth, NH: Butterworth-Heinemann.

Dryden, G. and J. Vos. 1994. *The learning revolution.* Austin, TX: Jalmar Press.

Duckworth, L. 2001. Oxygen and glucose 'boost brain power.' *The Independent.* http://www.independent.co.uk/life-style/health-and-families/health-news/oxygen-and-glucose-boost-brain-power-679982.html

Esquith, R. 2007. *Teach like your hair's on fire: The methods and madness inside room 56.* New York: Penguin.

———. 2003. *There are no shortcuts.* New York: Pantheon Books.

Fuller, B. 1994. *Buckminster Fuller: Anthology for the new millennium.* New York: Macmillan.

Gardner, H. 1993. *Frames of mind: The theory of multiple intelligences.* New York: Basic Books.

———. 2006. *Changing minds: The art and science of changing our own and other people's minds.* Boston: Harvard Business School Press.

Gartrell, D. 2010. *A guidance approach for the encouraging classroom.* Belmont, CA: Cengage Learning.

Gladwell, M. 2008. *Outliers: The story of success.* New York: Little, Brown, and Company.

Gowin, J. 2010. Why your brain needs water. *Psychology Today.* http://www.psychologytoday.com/print/49196

Harvey, P. 1976. *The rest of the story.* New York: American Broadcasting Company, Inc. (ABC) Radio.

Heath, C. and D. Heath. 2007. *Made to stick.* New York: Random House.

Ilibagiza, I. 2006. *Left to tell: Discovering God amidst the Rwandan holocaust.* Carlsbad, CA: Hay House.

Livingston, G. 2006. *And never stop dancing*. Philadelphia, PA: DaCapo Lifelong Press.

Logue, W. 2007. *Wordtoons*. Howell, MI: Education Illustrated.

Mackay, H. 1988. *Swim with sharks without being eaten alive*. New York: Ivy Books.

MacKenzie, G. 1998. *Orbiting the giant hairball*. New York: Viking Adult.

Maslow, A. H. 1954. *Motivation and personality*. New York: Harper.

McGreevy, P. 2010. 15 groups spent more than $1 billion on California political efforts. *Los Angeles Times*. March 11.

Oczkus, L. 2009. *Interactive think aloud lessons*. New York: Scholastic.

———. 2010. *Reciprocal teaching at work*. Newark, DE: International Reading Association.

Pelzer, D. 1995. *A child called "It": One child's courage to survive*. Edition Unstated. Deerfield Beach, FL: HCI.

———. 2000. *Help yourself: Celebrating the rewards of resilience and gratitude*. New York: Dutton.

Ravitch, D. 2010. *The death and life of the great American school system: How testing and choice are undermining education*. New York: Basic Books.

Reis, S. and Purcell, J. 1993. An analysis of content elimination and strategies used by elementary classroom teachers in the curriculum compacting process. *Journal for the Education of the Gifted*, 16 (2), 147–171.

Robinson, K. 2009. *The element: How finding your passion changes everything*. New York: Penguin.

Schewe, P. F. 2009. Music improves brain function. *LiveScience.com*. http://www.livescience.com/7950-music-improves-brain-function.html

Spragins, E. 2010. *What I know now about success: Letters from extraordinary women to their younger selves.* Philadelphia, PA: DaCapo Lifelong Press.

Tomlinson, C. A. 1995. Differentiating instruction for advanced learners in the mixed-ability middle school classroom. ERIC Digest E536. Available at: http://www.ericdigests.org/1996-3/mixed.htm

——. 1998. *How to differentiate instruction in mixed-ability classrooms* (2nd ed.). Arlington, VA: Association for Supervision & Curriculum Development.

——. 2000. Differentiation of instruction in the elementary grades. ERIC Digest. ERIC Clearinghouse on Elementary and Early Childhood Education. August.

Von Oech, R. 1998. *A whack on the side of the head* (3rd ed.). New York: Warner Books.

Wagner, T. 2008. *The global achievement gap.* New York: Basic Books.

Willis, S. 1993. Teaching young children: Educators seek 'developmental appropriateness.' *Curriculum Update,* November, 1–8.

Willis, S. and L. Mann. 2000. Differentiating instruction: Finding manageable ways to meet individual needs. *Curriculum update: Association for supervision and curriculum development.* http://www.ascd.org/publications/curriculum-update/winter2000/Differentiating-Instruction.

Zander, R. S. and B. Zander. 2000. *The art of possibility.* New York: Penguin.

Ziglar, Z. 1997. *Over the top* (2nd ed.). Nashville, TN: Thomas Nelson.

Recommended Resources for Teachers

I have trained teachers, parents, and business people throughout the United States on topics ranging from improving communication skills to boosting creativity, and audiences constantly ask me for book recommendations. I founded The Lazy Readers' Book Club (http://www.lazyreaders.com), which has ascended to Google's™ highest-ranked website for cool "short books." Go here when you want to read quality books that don't take years to finish. My mission is to increase interest in reading by providing cool, short book recommendations for all ages. From interest comes devotion. Subscription is free.

As teachers, parents, or adults, we often cannot find time to read for fun, and I think it is important that our children see us reading for pleasure. Therefore, each month I provide 10 book recommendations (three to four picks for adults, three to four picks for young adults, and three to four picks for children) that are quick and easy to read for personal pleasure. I try not to include any books over 250 pages, and I always include books written for a variety of ages. (Don't be shy about reading kids' books, though; they are my favorites because they generally have shorter chapters, bigger print, and colorful pictures.)

Many teachers who have attended my seminars have asked about books that may prove helpful or inspirational to them in their daily teaching lives. My first recommendations, of course, are always my books (as a matter of fact, you can find a pretty extensive list of recommended books for teachers in Chapter 1 of my book, *A Baker's Dozen of Lessons Learned from the Teaching Trenches* [Brassell 2009]). In addition, the following pages suggest books, articles, movies, television shows, and websites that have helped shape my teaching philosophy and are useful for various purposes in the classroom.

Books and Articles

Adams, Scott. *The Dilbert Principle.* New York: HarperBusiness, 1996.

Dickinson, Emily. *I'm Nobody! Who Are You?: Poems of Emily Dickinson for Children.* Owings Mills, MD: Stemmer House Publishers, 1978.

Dryden, Gordon and Jeanette Vos. *The Learning Revolution.* Austin, TX: Jalmar Press, 1994. http://www.tunetoddlers.com/page1.php

Gag, Wanda. *Millions of Cats.* New York: Picture Puffin Books, 2006 (new edition).

Homer. *The Odyssey.* New York: Puffin, 1997 (new edition)..

Linkletter, Art. *Kids Say the Darndest Things.* Berkeley, CA: Celestial Arts, 2005.

Mason, Jane. *Balto.* New York: Grosset & Dunlap, 1995.

Otoshi, Kathryn. *One.* San Francisco: KO Kids Books, 2008.

Pelzer, David. *A Child Called "It": One Child's Courage to Survive.* Deerfield Beach, FL: Health Communications, Inc., 1995.

Phillips, Karen. *It's All About Me: Personality Quizzes for You and Your Friends.* Palo Alto, CA: Klutz, 2006.

Reilly, Rick. Life of Reilly. *ESPN The Magazine.* December 23, 2008.

Retton, Marylou L. *Mary Lou Retton's Gateways to Happiness.* New York: Broadway Books, 2000.

Rey, H.A. *Curious George.* Boston, MA. Houghton Miflin Harcourt, 1973.

Reynolds, Peter. *The Dot.* Somerset, MA: Candlewick Press, 2003.

Schulz, Charles. *Celebrating Peanuts: 60 Years*. New York: Andrews McMeel Publishing, 2009.

Seuss, Dr. *And to Think That I Saw It on Mulberry Street.* New York: Random House Books for Young Readers, 1989.

Silverstein, Shel. The Poems and Drawings of Shel Silverstein Box Set. New York: Harpercollins Children's Books, 2003.

Tolkien, J. R. R. *The Lord of the Rings*. London, UK: Allen & Unwin, 1954.

Wooden, John. *They Call Me Coach*. Chicago: Contemporary Books, 2004.

Wormeli, Rick. *Fair Isn't Always Equal*. Thousand Oaks, CA: Stenhouse Publishers, 2006.

Movies and Television

Allers, Roger and Rob Minkoff. 1994. *The Lion King*. Buena Vista Pictures.

Avildsen, John. *The Karate Kid*. Columbia Pictures, 1984.

Bruckheimer, Jerry. *Remember the Titans*. Walt Disney Pictures, 2000.

Cannell, Stephen J. and Frank Lupo. *The A-Team*. National Broadcasting Company (NBC), 1983.

Crowe, Cameron. *Almost Famous*. Columbia Pictures, 2000.

Darabont, Frank. *The Shawshank Redemption*. Columbia Pictures, 1994.

Friendly, Ed and Michael Landon. *Little House on the Prairie*. National Broadcasting Company (NBC), 1974.

Hill, George Roy. *Butch Cassidy and the Sundance Kid*. 20th Century Fox, 1969.

Hughes, John. *The Breakfast Club*. A&M Films, 1985.

Hyman, Kenneth. *The Dirty Dozen*. MGM Pictures, 1967.

Judge, Mike. *Office Space*. 20th Century Fox, 1999.

Kleiser, Randal. *Grease*. Paramount Pictures, 1978.

Kritzer, Eddie. *Kids Say the Darndest Things*. CBS Productions, 1998.

Lean, David. *The Bridge on the River Kwai*. Horizon Pictures, 1957.

Leonard, Sheldon. *The Andy Griffith Show*. Columbia Broadcasting System (CBS), 1960–1968.

Reitman, Ivan. *Kindergarten Cop*. Universal Pictures, 1990.

Rogers, Fred. *Mister Rogers' Neighborhood*. National Educational Television (NET), 1968.

Stuart, Mel. *The Hobart Shakespeareans*. Mel Stuart Productions, Inc. New Video Group, 2005.

Swift, David. *Pollyanna*. Walt Disney Productions, 1960.

Winkler, Henry and John Rich. *MacGyver*. American Broadcasting Company (ABC), 1985.

Websites

Lazy Readers Book Club. http://www.lazyreaders.com

Newhouse, Ron. n.d. Today's Devotion. *Daily Devotions*. http://www.devotions.net

Science Daily. http://www.sciencedaily.com/

SingaporeMath.com Inc. http://www.singaporemath.com.

Six Word Stories. http://www.sixwordstories.net

Notes

Notes